I am your

JESUS of MERCY

Volume IV

I am your

JESUS of MERCY

Volume IV

Queenship
PUBLISHING COMPANY
P.O Box 42028 Santa Barbara, CA 93140-2028
(800) 647-9882 • (805) 957-4893 • Fax: (805) 957-1631

The publisher recognizes and accepts that the final authority regarding the apparitions and messages at Scottsdale, Arizona rests with the Holy See of Rome, to whose judgement we willingly submit.

- The Publisher

©1993 Copyright Queenship Publishing

1st Printing October 1993
2nd Printing March 1994
3rd Printing August 1995
4th Printing November 1997

Library of Congress Catalog #: 93-87010

Published by:
Queenship Publishing Company
P. O. Box 42028
Santa Barbara, Ca. 93140-2028
(800) 647-9882 • (805) 957-4893 • Fax: (805) 957-1631

Printed in the United States of America

ISBN: 1-882972-15-5

CONTENTS

FOREWORD

This book contains lessons, teachings, that Gianna Talone has received from Our Lord Jesus Christ, written down for publication in this book. The lessons here comprise the fourth volume of lessons that Jesus has dictated to Gianna; the previous three volumes have been published by the Riehle Foundation as follows:

I am your Jesus of Mercy		1989
I am your Jesus of Mercy	-Volume II	1990
I am your Jesus of Mercy	-Volume III	1991

Volume I, II, and III may be ordered from:
The Riehle Foundation
P. O. Box 7
Milford, Ohio 45150

Following the seventy lessons you will find the messages from the Blessed Virgin Mary to Gianna, and sometimes in Gianna's absence to Mary Cook, given during the weekly Thursday night rosary in Saint Maria Goretti parish church, Scottsdale, Arizona, from mid-1991 to early 1993.

During the Thursday evening Mass following the rosary, the pastor of Saint Maria Goretti parish, Father Jack Spaulding, usually the celebrant of the Mass, receives a message. These messages too are included here.

What should we think about these lessons and messages? Do they really come from Jesus and Mary? Certainly, none of us is obliged to believe that they do. Personally, I do believe that the contents of this book come from the Lord and his mother. As a Roman Catholic, I believe pending the results of the Church's official investigation, and I submit my faith-judgment to the judgment of the Church.

On the other hand, we can believe that the messages and the lessons are authentic, that they really do come from Jesus and Mary. We can read them with faith, take them as spoken for ourselves.

The lessons are not just for Gianna, but for all of us, for each one of us. You, reader, can consider each one of the following lessons as addressed to you personally.

I can hear Mary and Jesus speaking to me personally in these lessons and messages. If I do, Jesus and Mary will help me through the words they have spoken.

The lessons and the messages will help me to enter into a closer personal relationship with Jesus, and with his mother, Mary. They will help me to pray. They will help me to live my Christian faith better.

My suggestion: that you read this book prayerfully. If you read it just out of curiosity, it will not hurt you. If you read it in a prayerful way, it will help you. Let Jesus and Mary speak to you, in and through the words printed in the rest of the book. Listen to them. Let the words sink into your heart. Then, rest in that relationship with Jesus or Mary. Perhaps speak to Jesus or Mary in your own words; ask the meaning of the words for you here in your particular situation, now at the time you do the reading and the listening. Ponder prayerfully the words and the meaning they have for you.

Robert Faricy SJ
Saint Paul, MN
September 20, 1993

PUBLISHERS NOTE

The lessons contained in Part I in this volume started on October 1, 1991 and continue to November 27, 1992. The lesson given on April 3, 1992, at the Lords request, has been placed as the last lesson.

The lessons where all dictated by our Lord to Gianna Talone at the times and places shown before each lesson.

Messages delivered through the prayer group cover the period from July 25, 1991 and continue through February 11, 1993. These where either delivered through Gianna Talone, Fr. Jack Spaulding or other members of the group.

The following note is pertinent to the Lesson *A COMMUNITY OF LAITY* found on page 45:

Jesus of Mercy is not a community that would be affiliated with St. Maria Goretti Parish, only. Provisions regarding the community are to stem not from a central organizational structure, but from evangelical charity for one another. Any lay person or married couple in any diocese, with the approval of their Bishop, could live in unity of the community and still remain active in his/her own parish community. You may conact Gianna Talone Sullivan through St. Joseph's Catholic church in Emmitsburg, Md. (301) 447-2326.

The original manuscript calls for underlining to create more emphasis. In this text this has been accomplished by using a bold type face.

The messages speak for themselves.

— The Publisher

Volume IV

Part 1

LESSONS FROM OUR LORD, JESUS CHRIST TO GIANNA TALONE FOR THE WORLD.

MY GLORY
(St. Peter's Church, Rome; 10/1/91)

My dear child, you are never alone. I am always one with you — near you, guiding you, leading you by My hand. I wish to begin by telling you how so many people seek My glory, but their concept of glory is not of Mine. I am simple, loving, tender!

My people think that they must accomplish great things to receive worthiness of My glory. *It is in the simple ordinary tasks that you receive My glory.* It is not a merit received through worthiness. It is given to you because of My love for you.

I cannot say enough to you how I desire a great intimacy with My people. I continually speak intimately with you and ask you to continually offer My people to Me in intimacy, so that I can grace them with Me. It is in this intimacy they receive *My glory.* Too many of My people run from Me because they are overwhelmed with intimidation and fear of worthiness.

Please look beyond the materialistic standards created by man which indicate glory with worthiness. My saints are simple. I call you all to be My saints!

Do not allow people of man's power frighten you! Remember, I am God and I will protect you. If it is in the Will of My Father, it shall be done accordingly. *You only need to live in simpleness and focus on Me.* There is nothing more to be done.

When it is My Father's desire, His Will is done as He deems fit. Pray for all and live by actions of simpleness and loving kindness. Ad Deum and My blessings. Listen to My words now silently.

IMPERFECTIONS
(St. Giovanni Basilica, Rome; 10/3/91)

M y dear child, simply give to Me your love and focus only on Me. It is because of your imperfections in your love that I desire it so! Please, simply focus on Me.

The mysticism of My love stems from the imperfections of man, and because of the original sin. So many of My people are in need of inner healing from their brokenness and hidden love.

I wish for all to know that it *is not in the perfections of the soul I love, but in the imperfections! This is where you become holy, through your imperfections.* The grace comes from Me. Once you name the sin and accept it, I give My grace of healing.

The spirituality of your soul is a grace of My Spirit. I grace you with My intimacy. It is My desire that all My people understand that I do not wait for their love when they believe they are perfect. It is now I wait for their love in their imperfection!

When you believe you are perfect, I can assure you that you are distant. The pain My people have is because they deny their brokenness and do not accept the present condition of their being. They wish to control. When the situation does not go as desired - according to their plan - they then deny the situation and make circumstances to justify themselves with excuses!

It is necessary for My people to know that My Church consitst of the imperfections of their being! These are the people in need of joy and peace. First, for them to recognize they are powerless and cannot control, they must accept the sin and not place guilt on themselves. The rest is a grace I give to them for healing.

Thank you, My dear one, for receiving My love and loving Me in your own brokenness. You, who so much need to love others first by loving yourself, I ask you to sit with Me and attend to Me by focusing on Me. In this way I can heal your very soul and give you My love, for you to love Me as I love you.

Bless you and receive My peace. You will see that now many will come in goodness of My mercy. Remember, I am overseeing your journey directly. Surrender unto Me like a little child. Peace. Ad Deum.

TEND, ADORE!
(10/9/91)

My dear one, your tears are only healing from Me, cleansing you of your own need, realizing your need is Me and only Me! What I want all My people to know is that I call them to total purity with Me.

I highly esteem souls who wish to tend and adore Me, as I tend and adore them. Follow the way of My Mother. All of Her glory came to exist because of Me. How I wish all to adore Me and tend lovingly and tenderly to Me as She. How I long to rest My head on My beloved ones.

Times are difficult for many, but I am here with you on earth and in heaven. I desire so My people to adore and tend to Me. Suffering is painful, yet joy can exist because I can grace you with this virtue. If you do not have My joy, perhaps My purification of suffering in your turmoil is enough for you.

Acceptance in peace with trust moment to moment gives you strength to receive whatever grace I deem fit. Remember, you merit nothing. It is given to you. I am in everyone as if that person is the only person who exists in the world! So do not think some days I am with you and some not! This cannot be.

Oh, how blessed are they who quietly accept, without recognition and compensation for their efforts, their suffering when they feel nothing and yet, desire only to tend to Me and adore me! It is a true intimacy that the closer you get to the reign of God, the farther you think you are; and so you humble yourself unto Me, as I humbled Myself unto you to the point of self death.

Blessed are those who be lieve in My Word and **accept it**. I am not calling you to change the world through My Word. I am asking you to live The Word and see the world change before you! Blessed is He who sent Me, and Blessed is He who believes in Him.

My Father knows that anyone who would do anything for Me would never deny Him, for We are One! I bless you all My dear beloved ones. Come in purity to Me and adore and tend to Me, as I tend and adore you! Enter into My marriage without noting gender, only noting purity. Peace. Ad Deum.

TRUST IN ME
(Assisi; 10/13/91)

My dear, dear beloved one, tonight I wish to define the difference between longing for love and loving.

Longing for love is a hunger for love. Loving is living without deception. Most of My people long for love because they hunger for Me. But true love is not a hunger; it is a state of unity. When you love, there is no hunger because you are fulfilled; there is no deception! That is why there is much difficulty in modern world relationships; because of the longing for love. Everyone wants to be loved, but if you truly give of your own self and love, there is no longing because you are fulfilled and satisfied, refreshed with yourself for giving, rewarded, renewed.

Do you see that in the simplicity of My love for My people I teach them, so that they know how much they are loved when they give love in return? How I love to be alone with you temporarily as a lover would, only so that you can go forth and spread My love.

I want also tonight to talk about the Will of God. How do you know you are fulfilling the Will of God? *If you trust in what you are doing, that My Word will be fulfilled **by trusting in Me, not the Message!**,* then you are fulfilling the Will. If you doubt what you are doing because of insecurities and are not sure, then it's not of God! EITHER YOU KNOW OR DO NOT!! YOU EITHER LOVE OR DO NOT. YOU EITHER SAY, 'YES' or 'NO'!

If you, with all your heart, trust that My Word will be fulfilled, but because of other circumstances which were against your expectations arose, that doesn't mean the Will of God was not fulfilled. So, do not doubt. All will be done in accordance to the Providence of God, not in accordance to your desires. So, do not doubt.

Praise the Father and continue to trust. Doubt comes in when you look at your own self doings, and the plan on your map of architectural desire failed! Well, this would not be the Will of My Father if it went in accordance to your design!

Remember, He is the Potter, you are the clay. At times His Plan is laid out in your design, but most of the time, I can assure you that when you have drawn the straight line, He adds direction; and when your line is crooked, He straightens it!

So, be at peace and *know if something does not go according to your plan, it does NOT mean it wasn't the Will of God.* The Will of God is always done in those who trust. Self-pride makes you doubt the Plan of God or His Will. I love you, My dear one, as all My beloved ones. Peace this night. Ad Deum.

SELF DENIAL
(Before Cross at Lourdes Shrine; 10/21/91)

My dear one, as I was dying on the Cross, I looked in despair for My Mother in hopes that She would comfort Me and be by My side in My last moments of agony. She gave Me hope and love for My broken body. I could not find Her because the blood dripped into My eyes and My vision was blurred! In despair I thought, 'Where is My love to comfort Me? Has She, too, abandoned Me?'

All I had was then to abandon further unto death of My own Self, physically and spiritually. Those who are blessed to suffer unto Me, must also be crucified and die to their very selves.

Self denial is the ultimate self death route. Choose only to accept those things that give glory to God. If it pleases you and does not bring glory to God, then it is not self denial! Do not deceive yourself to think that it is. Be careful, as you get closer to My Kingdom spiritually, that you are not deceived to think that you are living in self denial when, in fact, you are not!

Self denial is an emptiness, not only of physical pleasures, but also spiritual! Avoid spiritual gluttony. Abandon totally in your pain to the emptiness of self death, as I experienced and lived out for you. This I have done for you, that I experienced even the abandonment spiritually of My Father and My Beloved Mother, My treasures.

Many wish to know the key to self denial. My answer is to *avoid all pleasures of self which **do not** give glory to God, and do not influence yourself to believe that, because it is your desire, it would always bring glory to God.*

Pray that the discernment and strength to self death, because of your love and desire to please Me, will always remain as the primary choice in your heart ABOVE your own desires. Accept only to live out those experiences and things which bring glory to God.

Beware, also, of spiritual gluttony. Allow Me to even strip you of spiritual enlightenment to achieve total unity in abandonment through self death.

Self denial is the way to embrace My Cross and die to the world, only to gain life. Peace, My dear one. Peace to you in My death on this cross.

THE ONLY JUDGE
(St. Maria Goretti Church in front of Blessed Sacrament; 10/27/91)

My dear child, never fear of My punishment. Fear of losing Me is the loss men risk when they denounce Me and do not desire the gifts of life.

I am here always with you because of My Love. The choice is for all My people. They decide which path to walk instead of surrendering to Me to guide them on the right path, separate from the ones they are taking.

Man looks for support of his journey and acceptance from other men. Words move them. They either boost them in pride or offend them through insult and shame. Those that know the Kingdom know that words in God and trust are the true ways. Those who trust in Me are not moved by the offenses of man's words. Those who are guilty mend their ways! Those who are innocent accept the offenses against them with offering to God. They are not moved for acceptance of man and acceptance of words pleasing to them, because they know it is I Who sees the ways of those who are guilty and the ways of those who are innocent!

It is I Who am the judge. I make judgment, not man. When man attempts to place judgment falsely on those who are innocent, I am the One Who rectifies in the Kingdom, the only one and true judgment.

I know the deepest incentives of each man's heart, the doers and the receivers! I even secretly place pretrial judgment to test the trust of My people; to see the depth of the commitment and devotion they claim to profess.

Today, My lesson is to tell My people that I AM HE Who places judgment. Do not allow the words of man to harm you. *Trust in Me and in My words, and My judgment shall find you free!* If you are knowingly guilty, change your ways by rectifying your behavior to reflect the goodness of God, by being faithful to My commandments.

Those who are innocent know that I am the judge, not man. Offer in sacrifice your crucifixion and be at peace. The grace of your trust has blessed you with the Kingdom of Peace. I shall come to your aid and be by your side at all times.

Bless you, My dear one, as I look to the heavens of worship and I proclaim to you the goodness of God's love. Peace comes in trusting and adoring. It is a grace. Peace finds you. You do not find peace!

Adore Me in purity without consolation, and you will be free always. No man can give you the freedom that I give. Hope always in Me and not the message! Know your state of being will proclaim My goodness, and it does not matter what you do daily to grant you happiness. If you trust in Me, you will have the peace I merit you. Words will not sway you, but you will be grounded firmly in the soil, and your fruits bountiful. Peace.

SHAME
(11/3/91)

My dear child, I came today to talk to My beloved people about shame. My people think they know what love is, but they do not embrace the love because they do not love themselves. The underlying cause is shame. Those who are sure to diagnose lack of love on their brethren are the first to have shame rooted deep within them disguising their own lack of love.

What is shame. When the soul is created, it is created the good in the light of truth, and purity exists. Man, through the venomous poison of judgment and resentfulness, places guilt and charges a victim, placing despair and embarrassment through humiliation upon the soul. The soul flees to safety, masking its charges, whether guilty or innocent, by avoiding the accusation and placing reason on another issue or even charging another person of some guilt! The soul is revealed without compassion or love, causing shame which metastasizes to other victim souls. Consequently, the love created is buried deep, and insult topples injury, and the soul cannot love because it is faced with humiliation from lack of acceptance from mankind. It is the norm of the society which exists throughout the world.

My people are not happy. They search for freedom by changing employment, habitation, in hopes of finding peace, joy, acceptance. Before man can be accepted by men, he must first accept himself and allow My love to cleanse him, heal him and dwell in him.

Do not let the affluent people who attach glory with wealth fool you into thinking they love themselves because they are accepted into society by society standards!! I assure you these are the people who seek the most acceptance and are least loved by man, in being, outside of monetary value. These are

My people who place shame on others because of the shame which dwells within them! These are My people who do not love themselves with the love of which I speak. These are My people who cannot be alone to face My love and healing, for they escape the truth.

Shame comes from the values instilled in man by man, instead of loving. Shame leads to chemical dependency, abuse, self destruction because of self humiliation, lack of acceptance, lack of love, embarrassment.

I call all of mankind to restore the components of love, mercy, compassion, respect, dignity and honesty. Peace to you, My dear one. Pray that love, through simpleness without conditions, will return through the openness of mankind. Blessings. Ad Deum.

LOVE IN HUMILITY
(11/11/91)

Oh My dear beloved one, I am always by your side, watching your steps as I watch all My people. I wait for all to be absorbed in My presence, attending to Me. Come and sit with Me with no thoughts, emptiness even in your darkness. It is a growth in humility. *It is better to have little knowledge and weak understanding than the hopes of gaining knowledge and wallowing in self-conceit!*

Reflect on your graces and the light you may have now. But what if that might be taken away? How, in your fervor now, would you react if that light left? I Who give light can take it away! If your light leaves, know that it may come back as I merit. Darkness is a growth in humility and trust, darkness to self-conceit. It is growing through the guidance of the Holy Spirit, paying attention to the whisper of the Holy Spirit Who speaks beneath your personal desires.

I want My people to know that My love for them is strong in humility. I AM LOVE BECAUSE I AM HUMBLE. I AM GOD AND I LOVE IN HUMILITY.

I do not need guards. I open Myself for everyone's love so that they can come to Me in openness. Are you so important that you need guards surrounding your pride and ego, preventing any risk of meeting humility? Do not jeopardize your destiny by escaping the truth. Do not run after the yearnings of messages and seers! This shall pass as everything will pass. Pay attention to Me and My words in humility. Do not allow your time to pass that is risking your security by not coming to Me in humility. I am speaking about self-conceit, lack of sincerity, lack of truth, dishonesty, lack of dignity, mercilessness, uncom-passionate self-injury and self-destruction through synthetic chemicals.

CAN'T YOU SEE THAT I WANT YOU TO JUST BE IN MY PRESENCE? Tend to your daily duties and responsibilities the best you can and **BE with Me**. Do not wait until you are confused in turmoil, and in need of assistance. Come to Me **NOW**, for later it will be far too difficult to focus on Me because of your illness of self-conceit and lack of humility!!

No one is competent of My love, but because of My love for you in humility, I make you righteous in Me. Must you always have an answer when you come before Me? Can you not come in emptiness and leave without any answers because of your love for Me, wanting only to be with Me, singing praises of love?

I love you, dear one, because you sit with Me. Whether I fill you with spiritual emptiness or fervor, your desire for Me is what I desire for all My people. Make your wish for Me this night, and it shall be granted. Peace, little one.

DEVOTION
(11/24/91)

My dear one, man places importance on spiritual things according to the standards of the world. My people believe that their wisdom comes from the length of time they have been practicing prayer. They imagine that graces will beget to them because they impose a value on their prayer which they feel they deserve - immeasurable gifts depending on the length of time they have been praying. Do they not know that I can do in someone in a matter of a short time what would normally take another years of prayer to achieve?

I am asking for devotion and commitment to prayer through the love of your heart, not through spiritual vanity. Pray for spiritual emptiness so that true devotion to Me can exist! Many practice their devotion when they feel spiritually comforted. This is spiritual vanity, placing value on yourself, imposed on you by you!! How few there are who are devoted to me in emptiness because few people risk the trouble to themselves to follow Me, and grow through the aches and pains of darkness where My truth of purification and cleansing lies.

I come to My people in two ways: one in the form of comfort, the other in trials. I deem fit what is merited for them. I rebuke their vanity and vices, or I exhort and comfort them with virtue. Be devoted to Me in all times of blessings or inner turmoils. Do not weigh importance of your own spirituality by the length of time you have practiced prayer, or what accomplishments you have achieved for others. I tell you to *be devoted to Me and seek MY acceptance, not the acceptance created by the standards of mankind.* ***I tell you this because the day is coming when the Son of Man will give you a warning of the bitterness of chastisement, where each man and woman across the world will see the judgment of themselves.***

If you seek acceptance and weigh the importance of spirituality based on the standards of mankind and its vanity, your judgment will be hard because your judgment will be the one you make against yourself. If you seek acceptance of Me and are devoted to Me with all the painstaking steps I lead you through now for purification, you will see that My path is not rocky or narrow, but is a royal thoroughfare of love leading to eternal freedom. Your judgment can be peaceful because of the love of yourself and for others THROUGH, BY AND BECAUSE OF ME.

The day is coming, and it is coming soon, when the Chastisement set forth from my Father cannot be escaped, but can be mitigated through prayer of devotion for Me. Begin Now. Love yourself now. Be free now. Do not wait or it will be too late.

Man needs time to change, die to the self made shameful through the lack of dignity and a burdened society, and be free. Place little expectations on yourselves, so that your expectations of others shall diminish to extinction.

Write My Words on your heart and diligently contemplate them. Man is cheated of his hopes, but My words are words of truth and everlasting life. They shall never deceive you. Have confidence in Me.

Remember your former ways and poverty when you were far from Me? Always fear God and love. Be devoted to Me. Do not imagine you can impose something on My Father because of your perception of what you think you deserve! Focus on Me and love yourselves and one another in My Name.

I bless you, and My peace I bring through My Divine Mercy. Ad Deum.

OUR LADY
(12/8/91)

My dear one, today I wish to speak of My Mother Who, in Her radiant heart, brings My people to Me in purity. She is the Woman of the stars, clothed in beauty! She is the Lady of wondrous signs. She is My Mother, Immaculate, born to give birth to Him Who was sent without sin for the salvation of mankind. She is Virgin conceived in purity. She represents hope to mankind. Those who plead for Her mercy flee to Her side, and bow down to Her. The angels tend to Her. She is My Mother. She is My Heart. She is all of Me. We are one in the same through the unity of the Holy Trinity.

You see, My dear one, all who wish for Me and My desires also give credit to My Mother, whether they are in belief that She is the Mother of God or not! Those who wish for Her and Her desires also give credit to Me. I love Her. My Mother is the Immaculate Virgin conceived without sin. Those who believe in Her believe in Me. Those who trust in her trust in Me. My Lady is the One Who, in Her simpleness, is clothed with My cloak. She is graced with virtues given by My Father. She sheds Her mercy upon you in Me and She, through Her shining stars, passes on Her virtues in My Name throughout the world.

There is no one like Her, yet so many resemble Her ways because She gives Her virtues to all for love of Me. I listen to Her. I listen to those who listen to Her. She is the silence of beauty Who whispers in My ear your loving prayers. I whisper in your ear My joy of Her love.

So, today, know that your Jesus celebrates God the Father's master plan for salvation through the Immaculate Conception of My Mother, the One Whom the evil ones flee from because of Her purity and beauty.

Bless you, My dear one. Make your wish on this feast day in honor of My Mother and in honor of Me. She will grant your desire. Peace in Our intimate love you share. Bless you and thank you for believing in My words of truth when so many doubt you and that which I have spoken in truth to you. The world will know of My truth in you. I will make you righteous in Me, and all will know that your delicate soul was created by Me for My Mission of Mercy you, through whom My divine mercy and love will transform you and flow out to all the world. Rejoice and never fear. Continue to bring all My people in prayer to Me.

I love you, My dear one, and thank you for responding to My Mother's call. Peace. Ad Deum.

BEHAVIOR
(12/18/91)

My dear one, in these My days of sorrow, yet joy, I wish for My people to know of the peace that comes from Me. I only ask for My people to be open to change, behavioral change toward their brethren. It is important to unite in the community in love, and that love exemplifies itself through change in your behavior.

If you are an abrupt, stern person, and I touch you with My love inwardly, you will certainly change inside as I merit. But to all the people who know of your past persona, they will only remember the abrupt, stern attitude and personality! They will not listen to what you say if your actions do not reflect your words. So behavioral change, one you are cognizant of, will eventually change people's hearts because the messenger becomes the message. I do not use you as an example here, but I use the person in the third form to be that example to which people can relate.

People talk and judge and desire, through selfishness, their acceptance. If you are abrupt to them, whether you feel they are right or wrong, whatever the circumstance, they will perceive you differently as if your behavior is not one of love, mercy, compassion, kindness and acceptance. *BE SOFT SPOKEN.*

I often say to My people, what does it matter who is right or who is wrong because man does not decide, only God is the final judge! So put aside foolish interpretations and being scrupulous of others. This happens when your focus is off of Me, when you are disturbed with desires of material self-worth. *Look to Me and you will take one day at a time, one person you encounter at a time and show love.* If love cannot be shown or expressed through sincerity and simpleness, how can your love shine to many at one time? Begin first with yourself. Make the effort to change your inner behavior and continually work at being kind and open to **every** individual (no matter what turmoil you experience!), and eventually your charisma will reflect your true self.

Peace, My dear one. I love you. Ad Deum.

OBEDIENCE
(12/29/91)

My dear one, today I wish to tell My people something about obedience. Those who humble themselves under My yoke in obedience to their superior are obedient to Me. Those who humble themselves initially under My yoke, and then lift their heads to go out on their own in disobedience to their superior, are exemplifying a hidden pride that has been seeded deep within them.

It is better to be obedient to your superior in the good works of God than it is to be directly obedient to Me! Pride can deceive, My dear ones, and many wish to go out on their own thinking it is obedience to Me, but it is only their pride they are serving, not Me!! When they wish to serve their neighbor, they are only serving themselves by pride. Unless you are obedient to your religious superior, you cannot serve any neighbor by completing the good works of God. It is important to make the distinction.

You see, my dear one, all good works that you or any of My people do, come from the grace of God. I am ready to give, but are you ready to receive? Prayer, discernment, prudence and obedience to your religious superior will protect you from deception from evil.

Evil can deceive through your hidden pride to expose yourself. It is like anyone who has the initial desire to do good works and serve Me through obedience, but then he or she decides to go off on his or her own and plays God!

Always be obedient to your religious advisor. This will keep you pure and poor in sin. The ox, who works under the supervision of his superior, may gather grain for the barn, when his head is buried in the yoke. The ox who lifts his head from the yoke may gather much grain, but will not have the barn in which to store the grain.

Pay attention to discernment through obedience. Take heed in silence. *It is as much a virtue to be silent as it is to have the gift of speech, far better to live in silence than to live in deception and pride.* I have given the graces of both through the gift of OBEDIENCE. If your spiritual directors say you are able to speak on prayer, then the good works of God will flow through you because you have first received the approval of your advisors.

My point to My people, as an example through you, is that if they are religious then they will be obedient first to their religious advisor. Being obedient to your spiritual superior is being obedient to the Creator! All glory and praise must first be given to God silently, prudently, obediently through discernment, love, kindness, meekness and humility. All pride must leave the body totally, fully and carefully, allowing the body of Christ in its full presence to absorb and possess the soul through purity. THIS COMES THROUGH OBEDIENCE.

Praise be My Father for His good works through HONOR and OBEDIENCE. Praise to Him, and as I humble Myself into the hands of all priests as they consecrate My Body, you, in turn through love, must humble yourselves to be obedient to your religious superior. Peace, My dear one. Ad Deum.

CONTROVERSY
(1/24/92)

My dear one, I wish for My people to focus continually on Me; not only when times are good, but when they suffer with mishaps. *The heart is humble when you do not allow the conscience to give testimony of your innocence!* This will not grieve the humble heart because he trusts in Me more than in himself.

My dear one, you cannot satisfy all people! Focus in on your own journey with Me, and I will make you righteous in Me. I wish for all My people to be at peace, even in the anguish they experience from others. Remember, I am your Jesus of Mercy Who will protect you and give you peace. *If there are those who speak evil tongues against you, then commit them in prayer to Me, and wait with patience and humility.* SPEAK LESS! LISTEN MORE! Your actions will speak for your words, and I, your Jesus, will protect you and calm all hearts in time. There is no harm that anyone can do by causing injury through words. They only hurt themselves! Never be afraid of the mortal man, but put your trust in Me. Be patient and humble. Look to Me, your Jesus, and I will deliver you from your confusion.

There is no need to justify yourself! Remain silent, prudent, and always discern in prayer when they turn against you. Silence speaks. Unless your silence would lend to an occasion of scandal to the weak, remain quiet and watchful, yet, always loving; but put to rest any fruitless fears. Think for one moment of what I have said. The truth is My words penetrated right from your thoughts immediately to the core of your heart and imbedded into a safe place, the place of My heart in yours, My heart in all My people.

As My people grow in their journey, they need to be watchful that their spirituality does not deceive them in vanity, or they only become thieves to themselves! I love all My people, My little one, and I do not want to see them use wasteful energy in anguish over controversies man can create.

Peace to you and all. Ad Deum.

SILENCE
(2/22/92)

My dear one, it is more profitable to hide the grace of your devotion than to esteem it through exalting yourself! It is true wisdom to simply be in silence and solitude than to speak much of your journey. It is those who follow the truth who look towards God and live in silence, without seeking consolation.

Silence is an increase in knowledge, a virtue of contemplation in which the spirit of the soul ascends. Silence is a whisper and grace of My Father in which He instills the truth into your being as you listen with an open heart.

Remember, the **Progress** in your spiritual journey does not consist of the grace of consolation, but instead, bearing the desire for it with humility and patience!

If you will allow your mind to rest and be at peace with simply being in My presence, silence will become your comfort in times of support and need. Those who are novices should be careful to be discreet and silent, lest they fall into deceit. It is better to be quiet and in a state of solitude than to see yourselves through your own eyes of wisdom, seldom allowing to be governed by others.

Silence will allow you to be ruled by God, and the way to flourish in the gifts of humility and divine charity! It is far better to be weak in understanding and have lack of knowledge than to be lacking humility and charity.

Humility is a grace, and silence and solitude, through divine contemplation is the catalyst to humility. Those who choose to be quiet through prayer and discipline, even though it may be difficult, are graced with true wisdom and lack of self conceit! I am speaking of silence, My dear one, **not being secretive**. I am speaking of developing and nurturing the soul through **intimacy**.

Quiet the mind and rest in Me. I will replenish you. If you feel far away and not rewarded, and empty, hold on to your faith and know that the light may leave as well as return when God deems fit! Better now for My people to be at peace and contemplate how it might be if the light turns to the shadow of darkness. And if you feel the light leave, know that it will come back. So hold on to your faith in silence and in the solitude of contemplation.

I bless you tonight, My dear one. In the intensity and depth of My Father's graces of darkness in your soul, you willingly write My words for My beloved people, even though it is of great difficulty for you. This darkness is one of light for your soul, and those I elect are graced with it. Peace. Ad Deum. IN SILENCE IS HUMILITY GROUNDED.

ENDURE
(3/16/92)

My child, where are you running to? Where are all My people running? You cannot escape the truth of life, even if you deceive yourself. Do not be dismayed with the works you have undertaken for Me, or of the tribulations which have come your way. Allow My PROMISE to strengthen you. Your hard labor and tribulations shall pass. Everything passes with time, but I shall never pass.

Allow Me to be your reward! So many of My people experience anxiety, they ponder when death shall be no more, and when there shall be never-failing health, infinite brightness and peace. Peace will come in a day known well to the Lord. Do what you need to do. Work faithfully and you shall gain your reward. Endure with patience and you shall see the end of evil. I will protect you. Come deep and penetrate into My heart.

You perceive a longing after eternal bliss, but you desire it without the shadow of change. This is because My people desire heavenly things without the temptation of the affection of the flesh, which they are not free from. So their petitions are not fully for God's honor. Break yourself from mortal desires, and allow Me to fill you with true peace. My words are strong this night because many come to Me with their petitions, but with an agenda.

The Kingdom of God is NOT an institution. The Kingdom of God is LOVE and encompasses love! It is not conceivable in man's worldly mind. *So step OUT into My world of love and try not to understand so much, as to walk by faith in trusting the Triune God.*

Oh, you people of little faith! Here your Jesus has been granted from the Father this time of Mercy to teach you and guide you, and you continue to act as if it is a myth. You go to your churches and synagogues praying to a God in a far-away distance; and, once again, I come to speak to you, but you ignore through scrutiny of the truth.

WAKE UP, My dear ones, to the true world! Allow the possibility to exist in your minds. This is the way My Father has allowed My teachings to prevail for you. Come to your Jesus and allow Me to come to you. I only want to love you and mold you in your imperfections, but you choose to be certain of what perfection is according to a falsified standard. Love yourself in your imperfections, and I will perfect you and make you righteous in the sight of God.

FOR ALL ETERNITY
(3/21/92)

My dear little one, how delicate My people are! I come to embrace them, desiring them to allow Me to love them and desiring their love in return. I am seeking a romance with them: an intimacy, not only of friendship, but of love. I tell My people; 'Trust in Me and believe I will care for you,' but they trust for the moment in which I speak and then fail to truly surrender all of their being in trust of Me. *I do not want My people for the moment. I want them for eternity.*

My people continue to fall in their trials and tribulations, but they do not allow Me to catch them! I wish for them to fall into My arms as they let go. I fell three times, My dear one, and each time I got up. You fall, but I am with you, if you will simply allow Me to care for you. I want to care for you. There is no fall, through your trials, that is too great for Me to handle, if you accept Me and willingly allow Me to care for you.

If you choose to walk your path alone, without allowing Me to help you, it will be a different and perhaps lonely walk. But even then, know I will be with you because of My love. You are NEVER alone. I see all, and I am with My people always. They are never alone. They may not allow Me to love them or help them, but I am still loving them and am always there!

I AM YOUR GOD. As many of My people will be firm in criticizing My words through their skepticism, saying My words are not theologically sound, I will still love them and I will continue to ask them if they will allow Me to teach them and care for them!

The time will come, My little one, when My people will know that *the truth is that they are powerless without Me, and it is I Who gives to them everything, even allowing their control.* They will soon realize, for the time is sure to arrive, that they, themselves, are completely helpless by their own merits; and they will realize that by surrendering and ALLOW-ING Me to care for them as their spouse, their fear, turmoil and suffering will end in true peace and joy and total happiness.

Bless you, My little one. Peace.

DRYNESS OF THE DESERT
(5/2/92)

M y dear one, in the heat of a hot summer, looking out into the desert, you feel the dry, hot wind beat against your face, and the stillness makes you wonder in the torturous heat how there is life. You begin to thirst and your skin begins to become dry and scorched. Where is the beauty of the desert, you say. Where are the milky cacti and the budding flowers with bees suckling the honey?

Your soul, empty, is searching for coolness and fluid to drink. Where is my God, you wonder, to refresh me and calm my mind. Where is the gentle breeze of my Jesus? You pray, you wait, you pray again. You wait...you pray...no answer. Now you exert anger and more energy. Your tears begin to stream down your searching, thirsty soul, fighting control. You wait. You wait, and you wait! Then in silence you surrender, realizing you are exerting energy without result. You accept, and now you pray without words.

The clouds now begin to cover the heated sun. Exhausted, you relax and close your eyes. The sweat streaming becomes your cooling source. The warm breeze brings a soft and gentle freshness. You fall into a peaceful sleep.

My dear one, what I have described here is how the soul in dryness exerts every last energy in the heat of searching for water to drink, in order to revive itself to life. It is the walk of the night where the light is so strong it blinds you, and you become anxious because the beauty of life is taken away. So, what do you do? You exert all your energy in attempting to find that beauty and, in the process, you become exhausted. The sun is so hot, it dries every source of energy from you. You become more thirsty!

In trying to control the situation, searching for freedom of spirit, you have found not life, but the opposite. Finally, in surrendering, peace and freedom, the cool breeze and freshness comes from God to restore you. The desert becomes a garden of beauty. The mountains shadow the desert and illuminate their lavender softness with the sunset! Everything that you thought was dying from the scorch of the heat is now clearly the radiance of the beauty of the desert.

My point of this lesson, My dear one, is to teach My people *to be still, quiet, silent, in dryness of the soul.* WAIT PATIENTLY for God to show His face to you. Do not be afraid; do not be anxious. You are not alone. Submit in surrender and in acceptance of yourself. Strip open your soul. Lay bare. Be humble. Remember, humility is grounded in silence. WAIT, as

I have waited. Look within. Be simple. Do not battle with control. Do you walk against a sand storm, or do you find refuge and keep still. You cannot control a sand storm! And so is the soul in dryness. It cannot control. Control will only delay by causing more blindness. WAIT FOR THE DAWN. WAIT. DAWN WILL COME, and all will be renewed.

Bless you, My sweet one. Here is the honey now for you to suckle and nurture your soul in God's love. Here is the honey for all My people. HERE I AM. Peace.

MORE PATIENCE
(5/17/92)

My dear little one, I am your Jesus of Mercy Who comes to embrace your soul, to love, to guide, to teach, to protect and to comfort. I am here with you now, desiring to give another lesson to the people of My heart. I shall continue to speak My words and dictate them to you as long as My people continue to listen and work on overcoming their obstacles by surrendering to the truth, accepting My love and guidance.

I wish tonight, My little one, to continue on the topic of patience. I have mentioned patience before, but now I wish to speak further on the subject. I wish for My people to bear their tribulations with patience. Bear the offenses against you for God's sake, your neighbor's sake and the sake of yourself. *Whatever good or evil you do, you do for or against yourself!*

Have compassion on those who do evil against you. Have compassion on their sins. If they do good, offer it to God. If they do bad, pray for them; have compassion and try to help them. When someone competes with you, lose if you want to win! The way of salvation is in the way of losing. If someone speaks ill of you, bear with patience and help him by speaking worse of yourself. If someone offends you, bear it patiently for the love of God and in remission of your sins. Do not offend anyone! Bear patiently without complaining.

You are blessed, those who keep their sins and the goodness of God before their eyes. Do not expect God to reward you. Blessed are you who do not seek consolation from man or seek justice! Remember, holy men do good and suffer evil. It is far greater to suffer and bear patiently an offense against you than to fast and mortify yourself. What good would it do to fast and then seek justice for an offense, even if invalid or not true?

Those who bear their tribulations with patience always keep their sins before their eyes, and therefore, are not weakened. It is a great virtue to overcome yourself. Look at yourself and continually work in yourself, on yourself and for yourself, seeking spiritual consolations. If you overcome yourself, you will be able to overcome your enemies. Just as good can be twisted into evil, evil can be turned into something good! This is all in man. Man has within himself things that only God sees, and so, can do good as well as bad, contingent on free will.

Therefore, I say to not seek justice or a reward when someone has done an injustice or offense against you. You all have sin and the right to be purified. The quicker you embrace patience, the less you will suffer and will be saved. *Look to God, only seek only God, not reward or consolation from anyone under Heaven.* Do not complain. If you are weak in patience and complain, the more you will be burdened. Fight against vices and treat tribulations and humiliations with patience. Bow under holy obedience, and the task will be easier for you.

I tell you this because if you are in a state of love, compassion, patience, no matter what destruction were to happen, you would NOT be harmed. It would not hurt you. The devils try harder to disgust you when you endure with patience, or labor fighting insults with kindness. You are being saved, and they wish for you to live in their own disgust. Whatever man does to you, he does to himself; so be compassionate on his sins and be patient.

Look at your own sins and you will see your own wretchedness, instead of seeking justice or reward. I love you to teach you! You do not love unconditionally and do not understand the mystery of My love. You wish to be blessed and saved without going through purification, self mortification. You do not want to labor. You want to be honored. The Father does not bestow His grace on the proud, but the humble! To be honored, you will be blamed in order to surface humility which destroys evil, and is the enemy to sin.

Patience is the virtue to tame the blows of evil through sin against yourself, and the offenses of others. Pray and endure. Fight against the vices. Make a conscious effort not to seek rebuttal in your favor, but look to God to defend you through your lowliness. Pray. Pray. Pray. Prayer is the beginning and fulfillment of goodness.

My dear one, be thankful I humble Myself before the eyes of My Father to teach the truth! My words seem harsh, but remember, My life is your Way! I AM THE WAY. I am your crown, and it is by holy patience you walk unto Me. I chose you. You did not choose Me. If you wish to walk with Me, you must walk My Way, not your way. Ad Deum.

If these words are harsh to My people, it is because they choose to walk a different path. All can make judgments on My words, but it is I Who have the final say. My Father asked Me to walk the Way for you. Those who are Mine walk the same Way My Mother did! So can you!! Peace.

SELF-LOVE
(St. Peter's Baptistry; 6/23/92)

My dear child, I, your Lord and Teacher, come here with you. As I asked Peter to make a final decision to follow Me, I ask you. You are a follower through heart, not so much in knowledge. This is why I teach you My truth through heart. I teach you directly. The heart lives My knowledge. My people may find it difficult to comprehend My words to you as "the" Lord, but I AM; and I choose whom I desire to reach all My people.

Living samples of My love I mold My chosen, no matter how impure. This is the way that My people can be certain of My teaching. If you were all-knowing, a scholar in theology or of My life and teachings, it would be unlikely for My people to be persuaded. But you are a sinner and impure yet in the eyes of God. I shall make you My love and mercy for the world to see that I am a merciful and loving God, pulling you out from the midst of your wretchedness into the cleanliness of My Kingdom, providing hope for My chosen people of Israel!

My people learn through patience. Those who put aside their selfishness can only then obtain self love in Me. *You must have a self love to truly love, but this self love is one which only focuses on God. This self love denies himself, and only desires to obtain that which God wills.* Those who truly love their very self will truly love. I teach of what this self love entails because it is not by the definition of this world's standard. The self love I teach is this: To love Me, at all costs, first above your desires. To be patient and to endure.

Happy and willing are they to rejoice in Me when all is well, but do not rejoice willingly when the time indicates uneventful fruits according to their standards. You wish to follow Me only for the moment when all seems well, but cannot follow Me with the cross.

True followers and lovers love Me so unconditionally that they desire only Me and the fruits from the vine, mature and ripen. This is self love and total union, not worrying over trivial ways of living; bearing with patience and being balanced and committed to My love, regardless of the times when things are good or bad.

Remember, I give you peace: peace, not as the world knows. Those who are burdened, yet completely abandoned unto Me, live in My peace. It is a peace of union, like having a meal together, breaking bread, moving forward and not dwelling on the past.

This is self love when, especially in the times of disturbance, that unity of the lover and the sinner is transfigured into unity of lover to lover. The cross then becomes the link between the North and South, East and West. The trials of the follower, through the cross, become the sweetness and fruitful consummation of the total union. This is when the self is purified to be found worthy in the eyes of God to love as God loves and to be merciful as God is Mercy.

Today I ask My people as I asked Peter and I ask you. Do you love Me? Then feed My lambs. Make your decision, your final commitment, and your confusion will dissipate. Then all obstacles will become the gateways. Then your desire will be only that of Mine, and then can self love commence leading to the union of the "consummation of My love".

I love you, My dear one. That is why I discipline you, to teach you. If I did not love, I would not break you, nor would I have been broken in humble resignation to save you. Let us now pray to the Father. Come, forget the past. Let us move forward together. Let us "break bread" and love in unity. Ad Deum.

LOOK WITHIN
(Jerusalem; 6/27/92)

My dear one, peace must exist in the cornerstone of your heart because I am to exist in your heart! Before peace can escalate out unto others, it must encompass your being in totality because I must encompass you in totality. This is the free will given to you through creation of mankind. You are only to be willing and have faith of a mustard seed, and I shall consume you in love!

By now, My dear one, you have seen what a mustard seed looks like, and you know the history of the parables relate in reality, not only to the people of that age, but also carrying into today's generation. You look for a quiet place of peace to rest your weary head, but you have not looked within.

My people need to look within. There I lie; an inner contemplation living amongst an active world. If I call My ones to solitude in hermitage, that grace is for those chosen. But most of My people are subject to living in an active world as I walked, and must flee within to find solitude in Me. It then would not matter where you are. The peace, solitude and love of contemplation would become the cornerstone of your soul, because I am the cornerstone of peace in your soul. I dove into the heart of My being, there to find My Father's peace and to dwell in solitude, then to rest My head on My Mother for loving care. You also need to turn for love, and care for one another.

The human needs the love of community and the touch of each other. Man was not created to live alone, but in unity. However, man was created to give glory to God for His honor, and so, praise to the Creator for His blessing was, and continues to be, essential for freedom.

Dive into My Sacred heart for rejuvenation of the soul. Do not look for rest and peace in outer sources. Look inside, and those who are willing to receive My love and peace will find Me! Here lies your protection and intimacy with God. Here rests total knowledge, the knowledge I grant you through the heart. Even though you have knowledge through the intellect of the mind, you have not knowledge unless it is processed and absorbed in love through the heart!!

My dear one, in My time of human existence amongst My people I worked hard. I was rugged and exhausted. I never ceased to teach My Father's word and to have mercy on those in need. I was crucified and humiliated amongst a market place of thieves and wild people, none who cared about the mercy of God; a common place where no one took heed of the presence of the Son of the living God.

I could not find peace exteriorly because the world did not exist in peace exteriorly. I came to save the world so all would have life and peace, but I dove interiorly into My Father's heart for solitude, contemplation and the peace of His love. I then walked the back roads to freedom by walking the active world in the contemplation of solitude and peace **within** where My Father dwelled.

I call all My people today to this same magnetic quietness of solitude, which exists **within** yourselves interiorly, not exteriorly. I live within. It is where you will find rest in your busy world. and the guidance of the teachings of My truth. Then you can see Me living exteriorly amongst all, but not before you have seen Me within, because there you will first see yourself, and therein, Me.

The Son of Man is coming to verify the past truths and to collect His chosen ones! *The time will come when all will experience the state of their soul. All will have to look within. It cannot be escaped.* There, where the peace of salvation exists, will freedom and protection lie.

Come, My sweet one, it is time to begin a new day of My Father's creation. I am with you always in your soul and by your side. I place My Angels of protection around you, as I send them to all My people of God. The interior protection I will procure. The exterior now will be guided by My archangels. Peace and Ad Deum. ❤

A CLEAN CONSCIENCE
(Jerusalem; 6/28/92)

My dear one, take down My words now for My people. A good conscience is one which brings joy in God. It is your glory when your conscience is clear! It is not in what is in your words, but what is in your heart. Speech does not reflect the interior. He, who has a clear conscience, will be content and in peace with himself. My Father sees what is within. Man looks upon the actions and speech of men, but it is I Who weighs the intentions of the heart. It is the interior of the heart which will ultimately speak the actions in truth, but what man does not see on the outside does not mean it is not seen by the eyes of God interiorly. Also, what man sees through actions exteriorly does not reflect in its totality inwardly! Man may not praise you, but this does not mean you are worse or less holy. Likewise, if you are praised by man, this does not mean you are holy!

My point today, child, is this: *walking with Me interiorly and refusing comfort from man, without seeking consolation or affection, is the state of an interior confidence and purity.* To do your best, yet to hold yourself in little account, will solidify union of a humble state. If you seek after the glory of this world, you have little love for what is heavenly.

Keep a good conscience. Clean yourself before the temple and you shall have joy. Remember, the wicked cannot have joy or peace because there is no joy or peace to the wickedness of evil. The projects of the evil will only perish. True peace and joy can only be sustained in Me, and I rest in the humble, pure and clean hearts. *A clean conscience is one who examines itself continuously to wash, to sift and rinse and clean for a resting place for its Master.* This means that great tranquillity of the heart will not seek affection of man's praises or dispraises, but will look to God for His face to behold.

Remember, child, that God approves and selects whom He desires to commend. It is not man to commend or seek praises or dispraises of himself. It belongs under the hand of God. Therefore, a clean conscience is one that looks to Me, to the heavens for union, and pays little attention to the ways of men and is not swayed by his word. Ad Deum. ❤

WILLINGNESS
(6/29/92)

My dear one, the spirit is willing, but the flesh is weak! All who come to Me can be strengthened. I have said that all you need is the faith of one mustard seed. Behold, those who can surrender to Me and trust in Me, can be molded and strengthened. It leads to the spirit being willing and allowing the weakness to reflect strength because I am strength.

If you try to live in prayer and in truth, love and kindness, I will assist your endeavors because of your willingness. The flesh must be disciplined to carry out the fulfillment of the word. This comes through willingness and desire, but also taking heed of the word through action.

I am the Word because I AM. If you have a desire to seek heavenly bliss, then follow this much merited grace. See with all of your heart that which brings fruits of the vine. The fruits of the vine will ripen from the vine. I am the Vine. As you have seen vineyards that bear fruit, only sweet fruit is produced from the strength of the vine. The way of your world is one which lacks discipline of the flesh to the call of prayer and unity, but reflects destruction through violence.

Look to your historians who speak of the past and learn that it is most necessary to **forgive**, and important to take heed of the consequences which could always follow suit once again through lack of unity, dishonesty and economic, monetary empires seeking control and power.

I ask My people to take the disciplinary measures to follow Me by living My Word. This is the fulfillment of the Word because I am the Word and I fulfilled the law of Him Who sent Me. Please, please take note of your indigent ways, and pray to the living God. Liken to Me by following My Word and living it. Study the Word. Be a scholar through simpleness and desire to know the Word. You cannot know the Word if you do not hear the Word. Do not be willing only in spirit. Be disciplined to be strong in flesh by taking the steps to live it!

I love you, My dear one, and I love those who are so much seeking life because I am Life! The shepherd loves all His sheep. Look at the true meaning of the parable of the shepherd. It has always been the same as yesteryears. The Shepherd still lives! Thank you, My dear one, for the commitment to My love. I thank all My people who are committed in love. This is where the living vessels become the Living Word. Peace to you. Ad Deum. ♥

SEEK ONLY ME
(Assisi; 7/4/92)

My dear one, look to console instead of being consoled. Do not look to hear words of yourself and your actions that would please you! Look to be at the assistance of others.

I am your Lord Who, at this time, desires that My chosen **forget themselves** and tend to Me! Quiet the mind and acknowledge how unproductive it is to seek consolation from others. You need to seek only Me. It delays your journey when you desire a human to support or evaluate your spiritual performance, when only the eyes of God can see your interior motives!

I wish for My people to reflect upon this. *If I am at your center, then there is no need to hear words of people's praise only to fill a momentary pleasure.* This is selfishness, and should be avoided! It is detrimental to anyone's growth, hurts and sufferings included. Seek to serve others. Listen, pray and achieve all that is good through serving others and listening to their painful cries. This will turn into your consolation.

When I say to forget yourselves, I am speaking of loving Me by denying your humanness, in order that I may live in union with your willingness. There are many of My people who live in pain, and are in need of love, and the embrace of comfort. Console these, My people. You are gathered to be in community to love and console one another in times of need and care. But do not SEEK consolation from others, as it relates to praises, yet graciously accept it when it comes. Simply avoid seeking after it, but console others. It is not as important to be understood as to understand, because if you live in Me and I in you, then you are understood by God.

Remember, through Him all things came to be, and apart from Him nothing came to be. *It is only He you need to love. I understand because **I AM THE WORD WHO BECAME FLESH.***

Let your spirit exalt in your Savior and put to rest your human behaviors, desiring praises of humans. I love My people. ALL WHO LIVE THE WORD ARE CHOSEN! Remember, you did not choose Me; it is I Who chose you. Those who know the Word know they did not choose, but were chosen. Peace, My dear one. Ad Deum.

MORAL DECAY
(Park Regina Margharita; 7/6/92)

My dear one, I speak now words for My people in order that they do not become discouraged, but will have hope in their God, for I will not abandon them.

In your world today, there exists much strife. There is the inequality of man. The rich are richer, the poor are the poorest of poor. There exists the fear of destruction, if not by military force, then by socio-economic or human means. There exists hunger, pain, suffering and devastating illnesses. There is much evil, both physical and moral, which makes the world entangled with greater tensions and contradictions. It has become a threat to human freedom and leads to uneasiness.

The church shares in this uneasiness where moral issues exist, fundamental human cultures splitting, and the depth of the dichotomy stemming from man himself. People feel alienated. This results in "desacralization", where nothing is sacred. The suffering of moral decay, in spite of the appearances of men, results in dehumanization, which affects society and humanity.

But I come still to encourage you to unity because the grace and center of mercy is My Mother Who has known the depth and breadth of My Way through My death. It is She Who understands the mysticism of the Cross which man cannot fully embrace.

Mercy flows out to those who seek mercy. I am Mercy. My Mother is your Mother of Mercy. She displays Her virtue of hope. She is love because I AM LOVE, and all who live in this love, live in Me through Her. She is your Mother of Comfort, Grace and Elegance: the most perfect incarnation of equality and justice!!

Those who are merciful know mercy. Those who are merciful know love. Help each other, My dear people and unite. My love exists in all. There should not have to exist two ends of a spectrum, but equality! You are all so worried about your own selves that you fail to truly see yourself. If you see others in their holiness and light, by serving, assisting, giving and helping, you will be tending to your very own needs.

Be sensitive to the poor, the hungry, the dying who only know the reality of loneliness and darkness. Free yourselves interiorly by striving for equality and freedom for all.

I love you, My dear people, whether you believe in My words or not! The truth in My words follow that which I have lived for your life and freedom. I do not force you to listen and accept these as My words, but the day will come that you will know these words are truth, FOR I AM TRUTH! Nothing I have said is against My teachings of My time. Focus on living My word, uniting in freedom and equality instead of expending your energy on analyzing the truth and validity.

If you live My Way, you can be sure you are living My truth. Allow your actions to speak My truth and verify the AUTHENTICITY of love you claim as your own. Peace to you. Ad Deum. ❤

PRAISE THE FATHER
(Inside the cave grotto of St. Ruffino, Assisi; 7/7/92)

My dear child, here is My place of refuge. The choir of birds chant their love songs to God. My Francis relied upon My Ruffino, for he had the grace of true contemplation and joy. Here, now, you pray and take My words for My people.

Sing to God the Father, My beloved people, love chants and praises. Absorb the presence of the joy He gives to the creatures of the earth, which you have inherited until you claim your inheritance of heaven. Safe and sound are the good fruits of the land God preserves for you. Rejoice in Him! Never cease rejoicing, for He gives even in your sinfulness.

Seek the quiet intimacy of truth and joy through contemplation and prayer of thanksgiving to your Father. He is good, as I am good because of Him. Because of Him, I am! *Those who live in truth of the Word, in love of Him, need never fear because they are forever safe in Him. Through His Name alone they claim safety.*

Rejoice. Rejoice. Rejoice.

Peace lives in the truth of His Word; Peace lives in Him. He is the Word. I am the Word because of Him Who sent Me. Blessed be My Father. Blessed be the Gloria of songs. Blessed be My Spirit, the Holy Spirit given to you because of Me. I AM because of My Father. Therefore, *blessed be My Father* THROUGH WHOM ALL GOOD THINGS COME. *Blessed be this earth He has created!!*

All who claim His Name live in His righteousness and are good, for nothing can exist in goodness unless He is of God. The evil may seem good at first, but the truth shall always come to light. I give you My peace interiorly, even though, amongst the world you live, there are those who do not desire peace.

My Father is peace, and He has given Me to you. Be not afraid, but take courage and know that I AM ALIVE. I DWELL AMONGST YOU.

Praise, praise, praise be My Father. I suffered death only to conquer the world in order that you may have life. Praise to Him, for I have risen! You shall never have to suffer the depth I have because of My Father! Praise Him that you have Me and your life hereafter. He is Good, and you are blessed to know Him. Peace.

PRAYER OF JOY (Given by St. Ruffino)
ST. RUFFINO THEN TALKED TO ME INSIDE THE CAVE. HE TAUGHT ME THIS PRAYER.

LORD, OH MY LORD. I AM A WRETCHED SINNER
PLEADING FOR YOUR MERCY
ON THIS POOR SOUL.
GRANT THAT I MAY SEE AND LIVE
FREELY YOUR JOY NOW AND FOREVER.

HAVE MERCY ON ME.
I DO NOT DESERVE JOY OF YOU,
BUT IF YOU SEE THIS POOR SINNER
AS YOUR JOY IN YOUR MERCY,
I CAN LIVE IN UNION WITH YOU IN JOY.

BLESSED BE GOD,
FOR HE SHALL HAVE MERCY
ON THOSE WHO SEEK HIM PURELY.
STRIP ME OF MY UGLINESS.
RENEW ME IN YOUR HOLINESS.

COME, MY LORD, COME.
OH COME TO THIS POOR WRETCHED SINNER.
MAY ALL THE WORLD KNOW OF MY WRETCH-
    EDNESS
SO I MAY EXPERIENCE AND LIVE
IN YOUR JOY FOREVER.

COME, OH GRACE OF JOY.
COME, YOUR SPOUSE AWAITS YOU.
NOT SHALL THESE LIPS REJOICE
UNTIL MY JOY, MY SAVIOR ENLIGHTENS ME
BY BREATHING HIS JOY UPON ME.

PRAISE BE TO GOD. AMEN. AMEN.

TRUE FREEDOM
(St. Ruffino Church, Assisi; 7/8/92)

My dear one, once you have recognized your sins, the soul in remorse is in pain because of its powerless and dark state of emptiness. At this point, I teach you to give more of yourself to Me and not to yourself. Give praises to God by paying little heed to yourself and focus on the goodness of God. Bless the name of the Lord, for His mercy is upon you. *Do not focus on your sinfulness or the wretched state of your soul, but focus, instead, on the mercy of God.* Sing songs of gratitude and thanksgiving for His compassion and under-standing. This is the way I ask My people to live. This is living the way of God.

You are powerless without Me, and you are everything in Me. I live in all, so you are all in each other!

Man needs man. I have come for man, so all can reap the fruits from the vine. All the fruits that are sweet come from the vine, though, at first, the fruit is bitter, because the soil is bitter after parting from the vine. Special care is needed, and pruning the vine, and time. When the season is at hand, the fruit is ripe and is then distributed.

I speak to My people through you, a wretched sinner, because MY MERCY ENDURES FOREVER. It is My love that molds and softens the hardest of hearts. If My love for you is great, how much more would I give to My people. My heart has been pierced, for the pain of love for My people still exists.

Do not hide in your sinfulness. I am Mercy, and I will bless you and cleanse you in My mercy. Empty yourself at the foot of the cross, and you shall live and be made whole. How I say the harvest is rich, but the laborers are few. Collect the laborers and bring them to the field. Your soul's state of independence is not freedom. *Freedom only exists in total dependence on Me.* There lies your power. There will I be in the quiet depths of your soul, waiting for you to give of yourself, in order that I could only give back to you a renewed and enriched gem.

This freedom exists through discipline and obedience, obedience not to yourself, but to Me. You think you are all knowing of the right way of obedience, but all you know is deception through superficial obedience.

Seek first the Will of God. Blindfold yourself from the way of the world and seek freedom through self-denial, so I may renew you and make you clean. Then you will be able to live in the world, whole, free and in purity of mind and soul. *It can only be done through Me. It is the only way.*

I AM THE WAY. He who knows Me knows the Way! Peace, My little one. Remember, there is nothing of this world you should be afraid for people to see while being stripped and purified, because I am He Who grants eternal life. I am the Judge, not the people you live around. Therefore, if all pay heed to the truth of the Word, all shall be purified and safe, because MY MERCY ENDURES FOREVER. Ad Deum.

SOLITUDE
(*Livorgna; 7/9/92*)

M y dear one, the soul is in so much need of solitude, a time to search self and live in the silence of the truth. Retreat inwardly to find the source of this grace. It is only through prayer that this grace is granted. How loud the whisper of the wind becomes, echoing and breathing life. So is My Spirit! It is good to reflect on your state, facing all imperfections with no place to hide. This is where union begins, knowing you are nothing and experiencing, by the purification of desolation and nothingness, that you can become everything in Me.

When the soul thirsts for life, because it is stripped of sensory and spiritual life, is when it has the graces of union and gives glory to the Father. God makes His union with you. Seek to find God through the praises of spiritual prayers. *Deprivation of the spirit from worldly attachments will come to ALL who are joined in union with Me.* The sinfulness of human attachments to the world through the senses and spirit must be stripped, purified and made whole if union is to exist, and for God to find His resting place within.

See the beauty in the simplest of God's creation. Be in union with the serenity of the earth as the forests draw their life from the richness of the soil, where God has planted the seed. Each tree in the forest is different, but all yield to tranquil beauty which the birds echo in their chants. Listen. Listen to silence. See the richness through solitude.

I love you, My little one, I love all My people, as I love you. Experience this love and see My love in all. The saints before you gave alms of offerings and penance, and their main message is still the one I preach to you today: to love; to give to Me; to give to one another, that those who are hungry and poor may live in union. *The richness of the earth was created for all, so that no one should go without. Why, then, are so many without?*

Give, and more shall be given to you. Never be afraid to come and be alone with Me! This silence of union is essential for the life of the soul. Even though your life of ministry be active, silence and solitude is vital and is possible. It is the backbone to any life of ministry. You must first face yourself in order to face others. You must first live in union with God before you can love others, or your life of ministry will only be short lived. Before you can go out to others, you must first allow Me to come to you and find My resting place through your own crucifixion and purification in solitude.

Now let us pray together here and listen to this silence. Blessings and peace as My Spirit of the wind breathes for your soul. Ad Deum, My love. Ad Deum. ❤

A COMMUNITY OF LAITY
(Assisi; 7/10/92)
(Note: See comment on page ix.)

My dear one, I bring you here to the first place Francis commenced his Order, even though this is your last place of prayer while here. I bring you here last, because it is the beginning of a life in My truth and love.

In this lesson I wish for all My people to know of My desire for a community of laity to form. I have asked you three times to form this community. It is for those who are not in the politics of the church, but who are the strength, the backbone to My church, the spiritual and those righteous in Me, My laity who are strong in unity and communion of love to one another.

The rules are established, but it is the spirit of love and understanding and prayer that will be the strength of the community; forgiveness and living simple lives; focusing solely on the goodness of God through praises and songs of peace and companionship; living the good Word for others to return back to Me, and also to live in harmony and love.

THIS COMMUNITY IS TO BE CALLED JESUS OF MERCY, and I SHALL OVERSEE ITS WAYS. I shall always protect you. There are many who have not been called to My blessings of priesthood, but desire as Francis lived, in the Word, in an active world of poverty, yet richness in spirit. This community is for My men and women not called to vocation of religious sanctity, but called to be in a community of holiness, sanctified through love and harmony through forgiveness, prayer, mercy and love.

I ask you this and dictate these words to you in a form of a lesson because I want to make sure there is no mistake of My desire for My holy community of laity. You, My child, shall be coordinator, not to command but to help discern those who are in need, and also to oversee the freedom of the spirit of the community. All are to follow the rules I have established, but living freely in the growth of the spirit, not through dictatorship but through love: to follow chastity, poverty and obedience, as related to community laws.

I NEED MY PEOPLE TO GIVE TO ME ALL OF THEMSELVES, SO I CAN GIVE TO THEM MORE. If My community is not formed because of your free will, I will continue to wait for you, and ask you to come to Me, to ALLOW Me to love you. This is an open invitation for you to follow and live My way, not only in a life of religious sanctity, but in a sanctified life in your world.

My people of today are not desiring My way. They have forgotten Me, and they remember Me as a distant God, not tangible or alive in their hearts. I desire for My people to come back to Me, but it is not by speech now that will be viable. Words mean nothing to the people today. Action and the spirit of the life of the community is what will be the proof of My words.

COME ALL YE MY LAITY AND LIVE THIS LIFE OF MINE IN MY LOVE. BE THE SAMPLE FOR MY WORLD AND BRING BACK MY PEOPLE THROUGH YOUR WAYS OF UNITY, LOVE AND SPIRIT OF COMPASSION AND FORGIVENESS.

I love My people. How I love them! and I talk to you here, in the same place I spoke to My Francis, because as My love and spirit lived then, it exists today. My love has never changed, even though the ways of time change. As My people believed the truth of My Francis, because of My words, they

will believe My words today, FOR MY CHOSEN, MY
SHEEP KNOW MY VOICE.

Ad Deum and never lose heart. Take Courage. Peace.

SILENCE OF THE HEART
(7/16/92)

My dear one, I am your Jesus now in the form of a
presence you are aware of but I tell you, I am with you
even when you think you are alone! Better to believe without
the affections of the senses to assist you, for this can only
deceive you.

I live in your spirit. I am in your soul. The soul, itself, does
not have feelings. The spirit of the soul is beneath the surface
of the senses. For this reason, I have stripped you in order that
there would be no mistake of interpretation of My Word!

My dear one, how good it is to have My people tend to Me.
How good it is to have you all for Me! You are tending to Me
in the silence of your heart; not only silencing of your mouth,
ears, mind and sight, but your heart. It is this silence of the
heart I wish to speak of to My people.

In order to have a clean, pure heart, there must be a silent
one. A silent heart is one stripped of the feelings of emotion;
but in the presence of My Spirit, which molds the soul, sus-
pends it in a form which adores God. It is a centered silence,
centered on God. You cannot see God unless your heart is
clean! I have said, 'Blessed are the clean of heart, for they shall
see God.' When your heart is silent, you can see God everywhere and in everyone, because your heart is pure.

If My people would quiet their minds, adore Me and come
follow Me, seeking after My Way, they would be likened to be
saints, My saints. It is My desire for all My people to seek and
follow My Way with the purity of heart. I hide nothing from you.

Silence your heart, and you shall see Me. I give to you all of My being , and I await all of your being! I will never force you because of My love for you, and the fruit of My love for you is My service to you. The fruit of this service is the silence of My heart! I am the whisper, the cool gentle breeze refreshing your scorched soul. Silence the heart and live in faith of Me. The fruits to bear all will be of love and service returning back to Me in My heart where My silence of love exists.

Always unite together and avoid disputes. WHOEVER IS FOR ME CANNOT BE AGAINST ME. I am the Word made flesh.

Peace, My dear one. Give to Me, My people, the silence of your heart, and I shall give to you a clean, pure heart, a heart that sees God. Ad Deum.

THE HUMBLE HEART
(7/17/92)

My dear one, it is the humble and contrite heart I will not despise. It is the heart that yearns for My goodness I will not turn from. I find pleasure in those who seek Me with a fervent heart, with persistence and self-giving surrendering.

A humble heart is a heart who loves what is heavenly in the midst of a humanly existence. A humble heart is one who always wills and desires that which is most acceptable to Me, that which will please Me best. It is one who seeks their will to be My Will always and follows it with a resignation of total surrender.

When I came from heaven for your salvation, I took on Myself all your pain, suffering and miseries, not because of the necessity, but because of My mercy, love and charity for you. You, in turn, must give all for all. If your love is pure and if you are humble of heart, you will be free and not held bound to anything!

Be at peace, and resigned to listen and pray; to do good according to the pleasure of God, and you will not be at a loss. If you seek merry things for your own interest, you will not find rest or freedom or peace because, in everything you search for, defect will always exist. *But if you are humble of heart, continuously searching to please God and tend to heavenly things, you will secure a lasting foundation, one seeded in great wisdom and purity.*

Things will pass away and even My people will pass away with them, but I am He who does not change! I understand all and sit in judgment of vanity and affliction of spirit. So come to Me, you of humble and meek heart - a heart meek with strength, endurance, not losing courage, but striving for good. BLESSED ARE THE HUMBLE, MEEK OF HEART. THEY WILL INHERIT THE LAND!

INFINITE LOVE
(7/18/92)

My dear one, My Mother and I are grateful for the work you do according to Our instructions, but ask now that you dive deeper into prayer. She will take you into My Most Sacred Heart. She takes all My people into My Sacred Heart, where My merciful love flows, who will allow Her and who are willing to give to Me all of their being.

Today I wish to express to My people My infinite love for them. I wish for them not to be discouraged with people who dictate through their authoritative manner and commands. Be loving anyway! Do not follow their error, but follow the way of My Mother. Listen more than speaking. **Love, assist oth-**

ers, and pray for them. Do not attempt to debate or be combative if you disagree, but do not allow yourself to be influenced. Follow the way of My Mother.

There are many who love Me, yet are accustomed to their way and try to persuade others to live the same. They forget that daily you must die to yourself in order that I may live in you and accomplish far greater works. Be open to the dictates of command, but do not allow it to influence you negatively. Focus always on Me and follow the way of My Mother.

No matter who is difficult with you, exchanging harsh words or instructing you in a selfish, authoritative command, you can maintain peace and harmony within yourself, if you dive into a quiet prayer and never lose your focus. *Do not allow people to influence you, even if you admire their ways. Be yourself by following only Me!* This way I can mold you into a beautiful creation in the eyes of My Father.

I love you, My dear one. I love you, My chosen people! I love you now and I will always love you. Never lose sight of the truth. Keep your eyes and heart fixed on Me. Follow the Way outlined in My gospel words. Remember, you live in a world of defect through sin and evilness, but I have conquered the world and died for your salvation.

In order that you follow a peaceful and harmonious life in Me, you need only to follow My simple instructions. That is to follow the way of My Mother. Listen to your fellow companions. Love them and assist them in need and pray for them. LISTEN, LOVE, ASSIST AND PRAY. And if you see error, do not be influenced. Yield to My love, My correction and receive My mercy through My Sacred Heart.

My Mother is the one who can lead you into this depth of My Merciful Heart. Pray for this grace so that you can dive into a deeper contemplative life. No matter what errand or job you do, you can focus in prayer, in love of Me; and live a life of forgiveness of others and harmony through mercy; following the steps through the grace bestowed upon you to listen, love, assist and pray for all. It will relieve your mind of business, and will inflame your heart with a greater desire to serve and live in joy and unity.

My blessings and My peace. Allow Me now to rest in your heart of love for Me. Ad Deum.

THE POOR
(7/19/92)

My dear one, today I would like to speak of the poorest of the poor. You live in a society of people who should live together in love, in union of harmony and in peace, but it is not that way. My people are poor, poor in spirit: lacking the charitable gifts; searching for the touch of love, acceptance, and the thirst for truth, peace, harmony. Even My people who have the gift of more than others are poorer than the poor.

First, look to your own family. Look in-house to your brothers and sisters. See how poor they are and charitably give yourself. Forgive and accept with love. Remember the way of My Mother! Follow Her way, and She will lead you into the wounds of My Heart where My mercy exits. Her way, again, is to listen, to assist, to love and to pray. If you begin, thus, first with your own sisters and brothers, then you can tend to the poor existing outside your walls. Then identify yourself with the poor of My people you serve, because you are as poor!

Share the wonder of My love. Remember what I have taught you. Your vocation is not your career or profession in life. Your vocation is that you belong to Me!

My people are losing their human dignity. My people are poor, and lack the desire to utilize their gift of faith. Serve My people. Give to them yourself! Give to them a humble heart of love. *Do not try to escape this path of love to the least of Mine, for you strip your own humanity of dignity, which will ultimately return, henceforth, back to you.* Learn from one another. Seek the face of God and adore Him in all. My people live for and by monetary means. I tell you to live for, by and through Me!! Give wholeheartedly of yourself. My people today are becoming poorer and poorer.

It is time for all to awaken to this disastrous devastation about to eliminate humanity from the face of the earth!

Please! Please, My dear people, you are all suffering. I have many lovers for My heavenly kingdom, but few who are willing to bear My Cross and serve the needs of others, especially My poorest of poor in the poverty of love. *Do not choose whom you would prefer to love, to serve; but, without prejudice, serve and love all* because, whether they acknowledge My love or not, I exist in and amongst them.

Only those who willingly condemn My love through their last breath condemn their own soul.

My love is enduring, and saves up until your last breath. Therefore, My beloved, begin to love at home, and it will be easier to love the outside. The more you love your family and all those you meet in your life, the more deep will be your love for Me. For you cannot say you love Me, and then not show this same love for My people. ALL ARE OF ME. If you love Me, you will love them, regardless of sin.

Peace to you, My dear people. I love you. Do you love Me? Then come to Me by loving Me through loving one another, and restore your humanity's dignity. Be no longer poor, but be the richness of life's breath through love!! Ad Deum.

SUCCESS
(7/20/92)

M y dear one, today I would like My people to know how I desire intimate happiness to be their way of life! I do not wish My people to seek emptiness or failure. I wish for them to be happy and at peace. Do not lose your sense of self. Use the talents and gifts given to you. *Invest in a success that is of God,* instead of investing in a worship of success through various means enmeshed in performance!

Lose your life for My sake and you shall find it. I am speaking of your human, mortal life AWAY from Me. Succeed in Me! Be last and you shall be first. This is an INTEN-TIONAL failure, seeking and following My Way. Not having is the way to receive Eternal Life's success! Your culture today does not permit for this kind of behavior. Thus I tell you, what is impossible with humans is possible through Me. For I am the Way, and I am Happiness, and I am Success! *Do not see Me as an instrument of your happiness, but see Me as the intrinsic way of life that you seek for your own sake.*

You are like fine cloth woven in My love! I ask you not to immunize yourself against your own failings. See it as a growth in My love and a growth in your humility to exemplify My love in purity.

I love you so and hope you will see that My desire for you is happiness. I am happy when you are happy! I want you to never lose sight of the truth. I ask My Father's protection on you because of your innocence. Do not lose sight of the truth or allow the evil one to pollute your visual clarity. Stay close to Me, at all costs, through your faith. *Believe in me, and failure will not exist because you will believe in yourself! Treat yourself as if you are Me because I am in you!!* Be kind to yourself, and you will be kind to Me. Love yourself tenderly, even through your failures, and you will love Me. Seek to serve others and you will be serving Me.

Love yourself purely, but do not deceive yourself and take pride or boast in yourself. Boast in God and, if you live in Me, you will live humble ways and boast in the pure of heart and tend to My lowly. Peace to you.

EXTRAORDINARY LOVE
(7/21/92)

M y dear little one, do ordinary things with extraordinary love! Have fidelity to the little things you do. Be at peace and believe with all of your heart My love for you, and that I am by your side. *Everything you do, do as if it were for Me.* Be proficient, yet gentle. Touch everything with an EX-TRAORDINARY LOVE. This is how, in your ordinariness, you become extraordinary!!

You must believe in Me and trust so fervently in Me as to be able to see Me in everything and everyone. If you see Me in everything and everyone, you will be loving, gentle and kind, if you love Me! For whatever you do to the least of your brothers, you do to Me.

See yourself as doing good. The image of the world has surrounded you through advertisements, and has set the tone of "good life". The only life that is good is the only life that lives, and this life is in Me.

See Me as your resource of happiness, for I desire you to be happy. Put aside your anxieties and absorb your energy in Me, which will influence a concrete response. Don't wrestle with your inadequacies, but embrace Me and allow Me to be the inspirational challenge to your successful walk!

Take the time to do all your chores and recreation with extraordinary love. You will never be left alone in this abandoned world of humanity. Come and see the creation of God through the eyes of God! Take time to contemplate. Take the loving "touch of love" to all your works and be a follower of EXTRAORDINARY LOVE. The people of your world are hastily working, and take care only of the things of meaning as they perceive; but all is meaningful, if I have created all!

Do not select only that which you desire to love. *Take time and love the small works you do.* You will find much joy and peace when you devote extraordinary love in the ordinary tasks, the small jobs done on a daily basis. If you can take care of the small items, then you will be able to love and tend to bigger projects WITH THE SAME LOVE. This extraordinary love will become your way, and you will live in union with Me.

The way you treat one another, no matter what position or title in life you hold, will be of the same love if you start to love all the weak and strong with a gentle, extraordinary care.

I love you all and only desire your love to live in the union of the Holy Trinity. My words are for you because My love is for you Because of you, My Father sent Me. He loves you. I AM FOR YOU. AD DEUM.

SEEK ME

My dear one, the fire of My love flames within those souls who seek Me. The indefinable love, which teaches and inspires interiorly, becomes the love which speaks outwardly. This romance of love is a romance with the Lover. *I am the lover.*

When you sit quietly and contemplate My words of love, your soul is suspended high into the abyss of love. You then dive into the core of Mercy's dwelling, the core of My heart, also the core where My wounds exist. The area of pain and sorrow is also the area of joy and love. Happy they who dwell in the house of the Lord where the Merciful Heart is exposed for all man's salvation!

Dress your wounds by dressing Mine with your love. Be graced with My affection, and persevere to seek the truth of My love. Rest, persevere, and you will obtain your dream of love Whom you cannot find.

I have not left you, but I am here teaching you inwardly, procuring a place of purity in which to rest My head. Tend to Me, My people! Come to My sweet abyss of love. Seek Me with the burning fire within your heart and never cease until you are found!!

How many of My people are afraid to seek Me, and they grow fearful. All that is necessary is a humble, honest heart, willing to receive My love as a brother, sister, spouse or child.

My dear people, do not give up hope! As long as you are of mortal body, you will feel heaviness of the heart. You will not always continue in a fervent desire of virtue, but do not give up hope. Continue to persevere and seek Me. Bear, with patience, this abandonment and aridity until you are graced with a deliverance from your anguish. It is good, at moments such as these, to humble yourself to exterior actions, doing good works and persevere for the glory to come. Not all can maintain a grace of spiritual ecstasy!

Contemplate how your sufferings now are minor, compared to the glory which is to come for you. In this light, you will be able to persevere, seek and love Me with the burning grace of My love. This is the ultimate peace and union of oneness to obtain. Be always searching the truth and adore Me in a Eucharistic silence.

My love is burning for you, and My sufferings of love for you will never cease until the glory of your happiness is united in the glory of the Triune God. Peace and blessings of the Father of Truth and Mercy . Ad Deum.

LIFE'S JOURNEY
(7/23/92)

My dear one, it is time to take down My words for My people, words of love and encouragement. My people will not be able to understand the full depth of My words I have spoken in My lessons; but, as they continue to read and study them, they will recurrently see how each word and phrase is designed and formed with great love in order to assist them in their journey.

The journey of life that you live is only the beginning of a long and fruitful journey of happiness. At times you feel that your journey is one of little meaning; or you feel lost, abandoned, or struggle with the meaning of your own life's journey. This is all orchestrated only to bring you closer to Me! All you do is not within your own power to acquire. (I am speaking of the many who attain their goals in belief that it was granted to them on behalf of their own merit!) Those who love Me achieve as is best for their soul.

Today you live amongst people who have little trust in their God. They are questioning the faith of the existence of God. If I grant revelations, visions or prophecy to one, the other closes his ears to knowledge in resentment and lack of acceptance. People place restrictions on their God: what Yahweh would say, act or do in others. My visionaries, prophets, saints, martyrs of today go unnoticed. My people refuse to heed the words spoken from their lips proclaiming My words of light.

My teachings do not cease. I am a teaching God, and My love endures forever. I do not change, and I journey with you. Do not struggle, then, when aridity and the thirst for Me is not fulfilled. I am bringing you to life's springs and endless gardens. The journey is continuous, but I continue to lead you through the darkness and confusion. I am with you, right by your side, and many times supporting you when you are weary.

This journey of your life is really not long compared to the journey of the glory to come! Therefore, I encourage you to *continue on with Me, even though you are confused, lonely, alone, feeling abandonment, and are not acknowledged by others.* I control all; and when it is My desire for all to know what should be revealed to them, it will be unveiled!

Exert your energy on Me, and put aside all worried feelings of anxiety. Allow Me to purify you from the tendencies you have to seek control of My love. Do not seek consolation, but seek Me, your Yahweh of consolations!

I love you and want your love freely, without contingencies or controls. It is a long journey of life I take with you, depending on your patience and your true desire to embrace the good fruits of this journey. Then, as you surrender totally, daily, you experience a true romance relationship, one fulfilling your life. Therefore, do not be frustrated. One day you are giving; the next day you are not. I do not get discouraged with you, but I test the willingness of the spirit and I teach you that what you acquire is not what you merited by your control, but by My love!! Peace. Ad Deum.

STEPS TO PRAYER
(7/24/92)

My dear one, I want My people to be in My presence of love through an openness. There are many steps the beginner can take in prayer.

My people need to take the laboring steps of coming in devotion and commitment of receiving My presence of love, even if they feel nothing! It is painful in the knowledge of yourself to commit in discipline to this love of Me. But those who endure to the end shall receive the flowing water to tend their garden with ease, so that I may come to dwell in it!

See Me, your Jesus, as your aide, your life-giving Source. Put aside your temptations of falsehood and sweet enticements of the world, and come to bask in My love. Be at peace. Let My love be the catalyst for your enthusiasm. Let Me be your teacher. Love Me with all the affection of your heart.

Do not allow the glory of the world to entice you away from Me. Pray for wisdom and allow Me to ward off the errors of falsehood which could dismay you and be a disadvantage to you. Allow Me to prevent all carelessness from affecting your progress. Be alert to these bothersome "sweet" deceptions. Pray and be strong through perseverance, that your spirit of love is not broken with deceiving desires and invalid arguments.

I love you and am teaching you through the Spirit to love Me unconditionally and to give to Me your total being, so that you may reap the harvest and be with Me in My everlasting love.

When you experience these temptations, pay no attention to them. Push them aside and pray the prayer I taught you through My Mother. **(Prayer noted at end.) Know that I am your source of consolation and happiness, yet this consolation may not be as immediate as you desire! *Everything must take time. Your soul needs this time of My love.*

Do not be impatient, but go at My pace, moment to moment. Do not worry about tomorrow, or the outcomes of events to happen. Do not exert your energy analyzing or discerning what needs to be the course of your life. Trust in Me, and I will care for you. I TRULY MEAN "TRUST." You say, 'Yes, I can trust, but God helps those who help themselves!' I say, 'Surrender and trust Me!' You are assembling an agenda you think is better than trusting, and are fearful to allow Me to care for you because it may not fit the dictates of your command. Oh, you of little faith! If you would surrender unto Me and be in My peaceful love, tending to Me, the fruits of your life would never put you in a situation where you need to discern or take a course of action to help yourself, because I would be paving the course of your safety and happiness for you!! But you are afraid because of the changes you anticipate (which may not even happen) with which I would strike you!

If you knew Me, you would know not fear but only love, My love. My sheep know Me. You are lost, and I will find you! You are running away in deception, but I will not leave without you! I am the Shepherd Who will not go forward, even if one lost lamb is astray. Remember, I have chosen you. You have not chosen Me!

Put aside your fears and temptations, and be at peace with the gentleness and loving caress of My touch. Peace, My lovers. Peace!

****Prayer Our Lady taught Gianna:**

"Jesus, I adore you.
In you I hope.
In you I trust.
In you I have faith.
For it is in you all things are possible.
You are Our Living God."

TOTAL SURRENDER
(7/25/92)

My dear one, as I move the graces of your prayer forward, you will notice one day in contemplation that you have progressed in this grace from "knowing" to "loving". The prayer of My love moves from the mind to the heart. Your imagination will be reduced until you only have the memories to remember. At this point, give praise to Me and know you have been graced with progress in your journey through your commitment and devotion in contemplating Me.

It is a challenge when you surrender your control to Me, but not a loss to you. You will never be cheated from My love. Your surrendering will only be fruitful and rewarding. The fervor of My love will inspire you to give to Me all the more; to give until there is no more to give and, even then, I shall draw from you! In this grace of prayer, you will discover what truly nourishes your soul. The search becomes the goal, and the longing for My love is sufficient in itself to sustain you. The fruits will become self-evident. The desert flowers bloom when your will no longer exerts energy to control or distract you from attentiveness to My Will.

The battle of the mind will no longer become an interest to you. Hence the desert blooms, because the source of nourishment is from the heavens, which showers and enriches the soil to produce a fruitful season and the best yield of the harvest!

Blessed is he that endures and perseveres until the end. The struggle of failure and success no longer preoccupies your journey of progression. You are now ready to open up like a flower to receive My merciful love and the compassion of healing graces. Your commitment to Me of your heart in prayer will gather the truth and will surface the self-deception of the heart!

It is the way of My sacredness in fidelity and truth. When you surrender to Me totally, you will be trusting in My love totally because total surrender involves trusting in My love. You would know of My love and trust in My love and, therefore, surrender yourself to Me totally.

Only when you trust in Me totally, can you trust others and respect them in dignity in My love. I trusted in My Father because of Our Oneness. Trust in Me in our oneness! Do not be afraid. Know of My love and know you will NEVER be left alone. *My Father was ALWAYS WITH ME, even as I suffered the abandonment of your life. Why, then, would I ever leave you alone? I would NOT!* I am true to My fidelity to you and I am one with you. That is why I broke Myself for you, that you would never suffer without Me in your brokenness!!

Rest assured of My love. Do not lose sight of My love through the fallacies of the self-controlling desires of the will and mind. Surrender unto Love against all self-comprehension, and you will bear fruitful virtues of life. Peace. Ad Deum.

FIDELITY
(7/26/92)

My dear one. I come now to you to take down My lessons for My people. I am a compassionate God. I will not insist upon My way, but will give to those who ask and endure with patience. Be persistent people of prayer, and consistent in your actions.

You ask and then you give up so easily! Where is your endurance? Will a salesman give a bargain to you if you do not persist in asking, in being a nuisance?

My love is not one that I will make you beg or plead for, but you ask in prayer today and do not follow through the next day because you become impatient and do not persist in endurance! Ask, and it shall be given unto you. Seek, and you shall find. Knock, and it will open. Keep knocking until it opens. When the door opens, walk in!!

I want My people to be faithful to My love through their consistency of action. If they pray and are faith filled, loving disciples, they will be consistent in their actions, service and love. All of this is possible for those who seek Me with a pure heart.

The heart, I have said, is made clean through silence. Not of your labor or merit do you succeed in strength of virtue, but through surrender. My love is true, but the tests I give to you to see your progress do not always prove true to your claimed love of faithfulness to Me! You want, but do not give in return. You ask, and then you become impatient that I have not responded immediately to your dictates. Then you doubt and give up on your God, which opens My wounds. How long am I to be manipulated by you to prove My faithfulness of love to you?

Give to me, and then you shall recieve. It is not within your own power to achieve. This type of claimed love is NOT love; it is not unconditional. All desire to reign as God.

How poor is the deceitfulness of your love for Me. Be strong! Take courage and allow Me to teach you the truth of love and her sincerity and virtuous fruits. So many of My people are stricken with pain and sorrow from this conditional love of deception and dishonesty.

Now you, My broken people, must allow Me to be your God; to remold you; to be the potter, or you will only continue to break yourselves and one another until the existence of your world ceases to be. Take heed and persist in asking. Be consistent with your actions in proof of the fidelity of your love.

Peace and truth be yours against the falsehoods with which you are deceived. Ad Deum.

GROWTH
(7/27/92)

My dear one, because you do not see your interior growth being relayed to your exterior actions, does not mean that other people do not see your growth. It is the same, not only for you, but all My people. Remember, you are blind to many things of yourself, and what I do outwardly through you may not be noticed according to either your understanding or expectations. This, however, does not mean that My works through you go unnoticed.

When you grow slowly, it is difficult to see the change at once. Also, this is for your humility. *The vices of the flesh need taming; and the worst vice, that of pride, is the most poisonous and the most difficult to tame!* It is not as important for you to see the change as it is for you to be open, to be a vessel of love!

"When you are in the forest, it is hard to see the trees." It is the same with spiritual growth. My people should not focus on where they are in their journey because selfish vanity can develop. They should, rather, seek the journey lived by My Saints as a guide to assist them in identifying the path.

Why is it so necessary for you to know the great works I do through you? When you are totally empty is when you shall know; but by that point, you will not desire to know. Tame this vice of pride now! I am not only speaking to you, but to all My people. You are no different than they are. The human vices need to be tamed. How shrewd the subconscious to deceive you to experience self-pity and need for acceptance and praise of your graces! Put aside these harmful thoughts and continue to simply live quietly in My love.

There is nothing you could say that I could not say without you! There is nothing you could do that I could not do without you. I molded you. I gave you the words to speak. I gave you the gift of knowledge. I gave you the strength and wisdom to succeed. So, as you receive, give back to me what is mine.

But also remember My love for you, and that I need you because I came for you! I was broken for you, and so much desire your happiness and love. *So, see My teachings, not as a reprimand, but as encouragement to face your vices and to surrender even more unto Me, that I may clean you and make you pure of your human vices of the flesh.* I will replace them with the spiritual virtues of heaven.

I regret to have exposed you, child, to your own inadequate vices for the sake of My people, but My people shall come first, and you shall be last. For I will NOT let one of My lambs be lost. The gems of My heart shall shine, and each, in their own beauty and rarity, have a priceless value!

SPIRITUAL MATRIMONY
(7/28/92)

My dear one, as the soul ascends in prayer, it comes to a point where I grace it with My love, and entreat a spiritual matrimony. You come completely into My hands through a void of emptiness which allows you to simply be quiet. I then fill the emptiness with heavenly love. This love is not a human love of emotions, as you know it to be from past experiences, but the mystery of the Divine. When in this state, do not fight, but surrender even more; or the current of the sea will only pull you farther away until, through exhaustion, you surrender! It is the highest, most pure form of ecstasy prayer, one of a union with God. No words, no emotions, no senses of touch, but an ambiance of peace like a baby sleeping in the ·

comfort of a mother's arms. It entails no energy on your part because the prayer of grace is all of Me, so hence, the purity of My grace prevails.

How blessed are those who remain free of their vanity to allow the glory of God to be their source of nourishment. I feed souls far beyond human comprehension. At this point, the beginning of your transcension will ascend quickly through My grace; not that you may be aware. It is not through your effort, so you cannot claim reward from your effort. But graciously give praise to Me for My goodness in ascending you in My love, a love I merit and emanate out to all I desire. Hear what you think you have grasped. It will be realized that you have only learned very little! What you have acquired is less than nothing; and so you exist in a tunnel of an empty void, not seeing ahead nor behind, suspended, but traveling like the speed of light in space.

If you allow yourself to allow Me to filter in My love, you will progress rapidly, even though at times, from the human element, uncomfortably! The discomfort is due to your lack of surrendering. When you have experienced surrender even further, you are no longer aware that you even have the control to surrender!

Desire only to be close to Me, and I will ascend you into another dimension of life, My life, where My goodness knows only that which is good, total peace, love and virtue. It is past the level of human comprehension. Do not analyze. Do not even attempt in fervor to seek more. You must just be who you are, not knowing who you are, but knowing you are because of Me!!

Come, come and be quiet now. Rest and listen to the silence of emptiness of the world. You will hear treasures of harmonious harps from the heavens!

Peace, My love. Peace. Peace. Peace.

THE ONLY WAY
(7/29/92)

My dear one, listen intently and hear the words I speak. For those who have ears to hear, let them hear.

I humbled Myself in obedience to My Father so that you would overcome your pride in My humility. Continually, you must resign to My Will and overcome your will and pride! Bear with patience for the sake of God the subjections of treatment from others. *Bless those who maltreat you.* Give to all who beg from you.

What have you to complain of to Me? Even in the midst of your sins, I love you and give to you because you are precious to Me. It is My hope that you will recognize My favor upon you. Be thankful. When I hide My face from you, shower Me with your love and praises. For I do not come at your beck and call, for you to realize it is I Who control, and am God!

As I give to you, give to Me. But give more to Me when you are alone and think I have left you! I am there, but I am listening for your loving prayers in silence. As you listen to Me, it is now the time that I listen to you in this silence. I do not hide because you have offended Me. You have offended Me many times, and My love still endures!! It is so you know Who is God. It is so you will surrender to the subjections of others for My sake, and that you will overcome your pride in My humility.

There are many of My people who, when things do not succeed with them as planned, grow impatient. Remember, the ways you would like to control are not in your power to control. It is not within your power to acquire. Those, who act as if they have been awarded this power, live only amongst deception of their own selves and, sooner or later, will be overthrown. Your worldly wealth and selfish desires to succeed monetarily through control and power are only short lived! The time will soon come when all must face death. And this death is a reality of life which no one has control over, only the Heavenly, Divine, ALMIGHTY GOD.

Live now in preparation to succeed in this death to life! You are but dust and yet, because I spared you through My death, your soul is precious.

Allow Me to grace you to be able to give Me the thanks for your graces received through My merciful love. You cannot glory in your own merit, but only in Me. Those who are wise know better to humble themselves in My humility, and do not extol themselves. Overcome, then, your will and be submissive in obedience to the one Superior, My Father! Those who wish to acquire glory in Me must submit in resignation to the Father's Will as I. *No one goes to the Father except through Me, and there is only one way.* You may exert much energy wastefully in attempting to reach the finish line through a shortcut, but only come to your own shortcomings. I have said, "Give to Caesar what is Caesar's, but give to God what is God's." *There is but only one way to the Kingdom, the way of love. I am love!*

PROVIDENCE
(7/30/92)

My dear one, allow yourself to rest and to give yourself with your whole heart to Me. Seek always to surrender to My Will. The secret of progress is patience.

Nothing will come to pass unless it is permitted by me. Everything shall be in accordance to Divine Providence. Therefore, put your mind at ease and rest in My love.

Acknowledge My justice in My works and give to Me your love. Have patience and take courage. Your comfort will come to you in proper time. Simply give to Me now all of your attention. I want all of you.

Trust in Me, and you shall receive the counsel profitable for your inheritance in My Kingdom. It is not necessary for you always to be preoccupied at every minute.

Just be in Me. Rest, work in the patience of love, and give to Me all of yourself. This is what I desire the most from My people. I desire their intimacy in simplicity.

Speak to Me simply, in detail. Tell Me the depth of your inner thoughts. Treat Me as your most secret companion, a companion in Whom you relay all your secrets!

It is most pleasing for Me to receive from you. Nothing means more to Me than to receive ALL OF YOU. I am a patient God. I am patiently awaiting My comfort from you. Give to Me what is Mine. You are Mine! I will make you forget your pains and give you the joy of everlasting happiness.

Do not place your peace in your brethren, but in Me, for only I can give you peace. You will become twisted in an unsettling affair if you look to please others for their happiness, instead of looking to Me to grace them with a bond of love. Without Me, no friendship is of any strength! For friendship to have a strong bond, it must have a true bond of love through a bond to Me.

MY FATHER'S JUDGMENT
(7/31/92)

My dear one, take heart to listen to the way I speak on the beauty of the world. Do not seek that which is of yourself, but that which is of Me. Know that it is at the core of your emptiness that My love encompasses your flesh of vices and changes your vices into virtues.

Blessed is he who hopes in the Lord. Come to Me in wordless songs and praise the Father for His everlasting love.

My dear one, I want My people to know that they need to be free of themselves! *Be master of the things that are subject to you. Never fall into being slave to them. Be master of your actions IN Me, IN My love.* Look to the heavens and always seek the Will of the Father. Always seek your help in prayer. Consult the Lord of heaven, or you will be deceived.

Many of My people think they have found the answers of truth through the experience of life. NO truth is found unless it is grounded in prayer. Why are My people so afraid to acknowledge the need for help of God through prayer? People become silent to the call of prayer and to the mention of the word. When you say, "You are in my thoughts", it is NOT the same as, "You are in my prayers!" Only those who are held in the person's heart of love through prayer are at an advantage. This is because the action, which is the catalyst for prayer, is love! The VIRTUE of prayer is love. You all form opinions of one another without realizing that all opinions need to be founded in love if they are to prove valuable. How many ways can I continue to express this to My people?

Do not spend wasteful time discussing the mysticism of God's judgment. This is beyond your understanding, and what can even penetrate into My Father's judgment? I never said you should argue or debate what is true or not true of My Father's judgment because you cannot comprehend it. This does not do good, but only proves useless!

Do not, My beloved people, look down on one another in humiliation. If you look down on one person, it will not bring you glory! If you take from ONE, you take from Me, for I have made the small and the great. Therefore, let it be made known that all who love their own way, and are caught up in their daily lives, should remain silent in judgment of others because they know not the way of the Lord! They only know how to gain their own glory against the TRUTH of the Word of the Eternal God.

Beware not to be a heathen! Regardless of race or church, give to God what is God's. In the end, with or without you, all that belongs to the Father will be the Father's!! You gain nothing alone, but everything in Him. Ad Deum.

LOVE YOURSELF DEARLY
(8/1/92)

My dear one, do not be caught up in yourself because it will only hinder your growth. There is a difference between loving yourself and being self-centered! You need to empty yourself continually abandoning yourself to the Will of God. Do not chase after the things of this world. Chase only heavenly desires, for everything will perish that is of the world. The more you strip yourself of your own will, the more of yourself you can sincerely give to one another.

Let go of those things you hold bound. Let yourself be free, and you will be free of heart! Then all your oppressions will vanish. Your fear will disappear, and you will experience the joy of purity and intimacy. Do not worry what people say about you. Remember, I can deliver you from any circumstance caused to harm you.

There is no need to worry what someone will say about you. Everyone must answer to Me for their actions. Anyone who hurts you will only hurt themselves. Do not waste energy on those who harbor hatred, and are your enemy because of envy and jealousy. If you exert your energy trying to receive the acceptance of your enemies by pleasing them, you will always lose! They will only sidetrack and use you for their gain. This is not an act of mercy for you!

Be giving to those open to receive. Be giving to those who cannot give. Be giving to those who are not willing to receive, but have a clean heart. Avoid the evil. I will handle their unfair and deceitful actions. Never be afraid of what others say to you. Simply keep your focus on Me. Do not do worry if you experience defeat. I will take care of you and deliver you to freedom.

Trust in Me. You wish to trust in yourself over trusting in Me. Those who love the things of the world apart from Me gain nothing, and do not know anything of truth or wisdom.

I am with you in all of your suffering. Persist, and do not give up! Stand firm in your trust of Me over the trust of yourself. *I want you to love yourself dearly. I want you to embrace yourself.* There is no vision that is of such great importance that it would supersede the love I want you to have of yourself. In this way, you love Me. I want this for all My people. I do not desire for you to be self-centered, seeking and chasing the things of this world, but *I do desire you to love yourself purely and keep me in sight, surrendering and continually emptying yourself in order to follow the way of **love, truth, hope and mercy**.*

Bless you, My dear people. Be at peace.

WISDOM AND ETERNAL TRUTH
(8/2/92)

My dear one, I, your beloved Jesus, come to meet you; to strengthen you and to speak words of wisdom and truth to My people through you. Blessed are they that seek the way of eternal truth and wisdom by putting aside the ways of the world.

Many of My people desire initially the heavenly graces, but soon abandon the heavenly desire for the enticements of the world. Place your investments in the reality of the Eternal

Word! I am the Word, for I AM. I am the Word made Flesh. In order to always be on the path to righteousness, you MUST continually decline the falsehoods of deception through the richness of this "man made" world. This "man made" richness will never grant you eternal freedom.

Blessed ar the wise who seek first the Kingdom of God and will deny the things of the world which would prevent their gain. There are many who begin their journey, but never find the path! They are the ones who speak of the way of goodness, but never practice those ways. There are also the ones who practice, half-heartedly, My words, selecting those to whom they desire to give themselves. These are the ones who settle for less because they will never gain the entire treasure of the Kingdom. They desire to settle for less and they will not be able to select the treasure of heaven!

Then there are My few who do not pay heed to the ways of the world, but pay heed to the ETERNAL WAY OF TRUTH. These are the wise, the ones who give the best of their ability without showing favoritism in their love. They listen to the Word and discern the Will of My Father in their lives, even if they make human mistakes.

Enjoy the fruits of the world, the beauty My Father created, because He created it! His works are good, and He desired the fruits of the land to multiply. But do not be attached to the world. Be attached only to God. Do not take for granted the gifts of the Lord given to you. Be people of virtue, and treasure the Eternal way.

Your desire for the goodness of My Way must supersede all human desires, for these are the ways of success. It is necessary to work always to achieve heavenly bliss. You will never be able to perfect your way, even on My Path! *The way of this life is only a breath of the life of perfection to come!*

Live your life now for the true Way of Peace and Joy to be attained through your efforts now in this world. Give of yourself and keep giving of yourself without looking for acknowl-edgment, recognition or repayment from those to whom you give. Simply look to the heavens!! Raise your eyes to Me, and I shall fill you so fully that you will overflow with graces and virtues of satisfaction.

Blessed is he who seeks the truth and wisdom of Heaven, and not of this world. I love you, My dear one. It is no secret! I love My people. That is no secret! I lived for you a human life; suffered a human death; experienced human temptations all for humanity. What you experience, I have experienced. The way My Angels waited on Me is the same way My Angels wait on everyone! But TRUST and have CONFIDENCE in your love of Me through the love of yourself.

Very few of My people have confidence in their love of themselves because they do not have full confidence in Me. If they did, the way of your world would be a way of love of one another and of peace and of joy; not a world that seeks joy through success, monetary values and power! My people trust in the things that limit the depth of happiness over the eternal heavenly things that are very real and long-lasting.

My words are truth. My words are wisdom. Happy and blessed are they who listen, follow and abandon unto **TRUTH**. They are my wise; and to them, more shall be given! Peace, my love. Ad deum.

ENDURANCE
(8/3/92)

My dear one, you will not be able to endure any hardship unless you have patience! In this world, you need the protection of spiritual weapons because you will never be free from different sorts of misery.

Bear all for My sake, but know that you will not always gain the comfort you desire at the time you want it!! Even My Saints endured much pain and sorrows. They were tested, and also experienced temptations. You will not be any different. It is the same for all MY people. Endure these hardships for My sake. Remove yourself and the desire of your self image, and have confidence in Me.

I will be with you in all your trials. Know that, when you experience anxieties, humiliation, disappointments, difficulties, temptations, injuries, sickness, endure them in patience. I will strengthen you in virtue - the graces to be held for those who have confidence and love for Me, those who do not abandon their hope in Me. My Saints all were purified in the same way.

It is so necessary to practice patience. Where are you running that you must hurry to the finish line?

Go at My pace. Face the obstacles on the road with patience and gentleness of self, but in confidence that God will deliver you; and you shall appreciate crossing the finish line far more, because your efforts will leave tracks for your beloved to follow!

Take your time! There is no meaning of time, My people, in Heaven, so do not set deadlines on your growth, or you may be passing up the beauty. Fuel is needed to get you to that finish line!! What happens if you think you've crossed successfully? What then? You cannot do anything without Me. If you cross, you still have to wait for Me! And after you have raced to that finish line, avoiding and darting around the obstacles instead of enduring with patience, your journey with obstacles will only begin!

Have confidence in Me. Be at peace and know that all journeys have crosses. They will include disappointments or trials of some sort, but take courage. Move forward in hope and confidence in Me. Give Me MORE of your love. Give MORE, MORE AND MORE! Give through patience, the surrender of love, acceptance and TRUST.

You want your crown of jewels without sharing in the jewels of the thorns! Take first My thorns, and you will not desire the jewels. Never be distracted from My love through trusting someone other than Me. Never lose your focus. If you lose it, refocus because you will NOT go unwounded if you are NOT grounded in My love through patience. I love you, so I teach you, to help you, so I can bless you with My virtue.

Be strong and have confidence in your God. *Do not run away. Walk slowly! The end of time will not commence without Me, and I will wait for you. I've been waiting and I will continue to wait until completely denied.* Peace. Ad Deum.

INTERIOR CALM
(8/4/92)

My dear one, take these words down for My people. It is important that you look to yourself and your way before you are quick to correct someone! It is necessary to take special care of yourself interiorly. *Work at being calm, and see that you remain focused on My love.* In this way, the words of others will not take offense in you but will only be words. Why do you let the words of others affect you so? It is because you are still of this world and have not given yourself to Me.

Do not let distractions get in the way of your focus. Habit must overcome habit. Habitually, love, and keep your mind fixed on Me. Remember, I see all; and, many times, circumstances arise because I desire to see your actions, not when all is well, but in troubled times!!

I have told you that if you want to advance in spiritual progress, you must put aside all trivial, momentary distractions and have a profound love for Me. Your feelings of aggression will pass, and you will return to a state of equilibrium. When people admonish you and tell you to be careful of your behavior, to be kind and to reflect what is expected of you, do not be offended! Praise the person who admonishes you by thanking them for pointing out the truth in such charity. Even if you already KNOW what has been said to you in your heart, thank the person anyway. It is an act of humility to not take offense.

Do not take to heart what people say. I tell you over and over again that words should not move you one way or the other. If they do, you are seeking to please others and look towards their affection with fondness. *You need to be fully sustained in me. I tell you over and over again! I have mentioned this in previous lessons. What can man do that I cannot free them and deliver from them?*

Your mortal life is but a breath of what is to come. But you continue to live in fear of one another. The way of mortal life is one that will always have some type of turmoil because of impurities, so why be disturbed? Seek to be confident and calm, and raise your eyes to the heavens to be governed. Then you will be happy, even in the midst of pain surrounding you. You can be immunized against the ill effects of human judgment because I am the judge of righteousness!

Work to maintain equanimity. Change you habits and adopt true habits that remain faithful to the Word. I AM THE WORD MADE FLESH. Peace My loved one. Peace. Ad Deum.

ROOTS
(8/5/92)

My dear one, I give to you My heart. There are many people who will seem to always contradict you, or be overpowering. Do not be threatened by anyone's words or actions. Remember, I am God! Be secure and confident in My love, and remember that I allow situations to happen for your growth in humility. Put aside your frustrations. They are not firmly grounded. The abyss of My love is here to comfort you. Do not run away from tensions. Be humble to recognize the need for unity. Do not allow abuse; but be kind and if you are not at fault, humbly express your inflicted pain, but do so without causing conflict. Be secure enough in yourself and joyful in Me!

Your spirit is free when joyfully it sings songs of love. My grace is precious. Put aside anything that would get in the way of My grace being received. Maintain a clean conscience and seek to serve Me. When you make a mistake and have failed, *learn by your mistake, pray in sorrow for your mistake and move on,*

Do not block My grace meant for you. This is why I have told you to look into the depths of your being: your chemical (i.e. physical) and spiritual and emotional makeup, so that you will be in union with yourself and understand your reactions with love in moments of difficulty. Placing your confidence in My love for yourself will allow you to maintain a clear conscience. If you place Me first, you will perceive My love as the most important value of your life. But the roots to selfishness and other human vices must be severed. This is painful at times, but *your persistence, dedication and commitment to My love will master your frail and lifeless habits and behavior this is how you begin to love yourself. I then become the center of your life, replacing you!*

Many people have difficulty with this and, because they are not willing to ascend to a purer interior state, remain trapped; and they build that cocoon around themselves and never rise to self freedom and love. The same is true if you are innocent of error. Remain open to My grace. Do not harbor any resentfulness, but *place your confidence in Me and remain in union with yourself in my love.* You will soar to the abyss of ecstatic union in the state of humility.

I love you. Don't give up in these difficult moments. Offer them to Me in the humility of My love for you. Peace, little one. Ad Deum.

SIMPLICITY
(8/6/92)

M y dear one, I want My people to now know the impor tance of simplicity. If your intention is to be good and pure, it must be simple. If you seek My Will and nothing else, you will experience the abode of My love; and the creations around you will be magnified in My goodness in your emotional and interior state.

For a pure heart is one that sees goodness. He, who has a pure heart, will experience joy because that person will see My hands in the sweetness of creation. But the person who has apathy for himself is one who experiences the anguish of life because he (no specific gender) knows not the state of interior joy. For what God has created is good. The pure soul will see this goodness without difficulty. *Taking care of all the little things of the world (for everything has value) in an intention of simplicity, ascends your soul in a transformation of God's goodness.*

As I purify you and make you clean, you may suffer the markings of pain from worldly attachments. Those who persevere and remain persistent in prayer, saturated in faith, move from apathy to courage, and are transfigured in the likeness of purity and joy. Life then becomes life! The fullness of color and the fullness of the senses return to appreciate and to unite in harmony with creation!

My dear one, each person created must stand alone before God the Father!

My Father embraces each person with a love beyond your comprehension. *It is necessary that my people begin to strive for an inner harmony of quiet and peace, allowing the way for the unity of the Trinity to enter and find rest. Begin through actions of simplicity and openness of necessary detachments from human behavior.*

My peace is with you in all the things of creation in the world. Nothing is worthless! Every creation is of value, and magnifies the illuminous love of God. Ad Deum.

FEARS
(8/7/92)

My dear one, I want My people to know to fear nothing! I watch your heart in great attention. If I am with you, who can dare touch you? In order to do My work, you must relinquish all self-centeredness and seek that which is pleasing to the will of God. This is how you witness the fruits of the spirit. I am pleased when, in your simpleness, you share with Me even your fears. This is good. Hide nothing from Me and you will ascend. Acknowledging your fears is fruitful, realizing that you have nothing to fear of the fear. Taming that fear in My love allows you to breathe freedom from the control of your crippling fears.

In order for all to be free and grow in humility and experience the joy of their being in My love, all must look at their inner state, praying for My grace to address their needs spiritually, physically and emotionally. Nothing is lost except fear! Fear would like to control you and deceive you to think that if you face it, you would lose self-dignity, respect, love of self and become mindless.

The reality is that *when you face fear, it is fear that dissipates. Call your fear. Name your fears and tame your fears in My love, through gentleness and kindness and, most importantly, through love of yourself.* Your energy will then be rerouted anew to a colorful force of joy and happiness of within your true self in My love.

You will see that, through lack of facing your fear, you were losing your love, your control of emotions, your dignity, your respect and clarity of your thought processes. It is a step all My people need to take, since only few have courageously stepped into the open abyss, and persevered in the persistence of faith and love by My gracing help.

You, My dear one, are going through this process, and everything I teach to My people, you must actually live. You must experience each word I speak in order for you to witness My love to all My people. My people can relate to one who has lived the turmoil, and overcome it, in order for them to listen to any authoritativeness regarding My love and Mercy. If you did not experience this, all for My people, then your words would only be words.

My people are precious, and all need the gentleness of love to replace their fears and brokenness. I am with my people. I hope in My people. *I encourage My people to take that leap for love of themselves and their God.* I wait for them through you. Give to them, through giving of yourself, My love, and My love will stay with them. I will mold them, then, Myself. But love conquers through union and harmony. And so, I unite Myself with you for My quest of this love of My people.

CONFIDENCE
(8/8/92)

My dear one, when a person who is beloved of Mine does not pay heed to acknowledging your own creative beauty and self giving ways, do not despair. Move forward triumphantly. Remember, all are created good in My image, but all are also stained through the stain of sin in free choice to follow the way of the world.

At times, even My most beloved fall prey to pride, self-centeredness and the desire to control and be ruler. When you are graced to witness this, and fall prey to suffering because of human ways, do not despair. Have hope, and call on Me, your Shepherd. *Take firmly the hands of this suffering and sorrow, but do not choose to grasp the hands of pride or hatred to deceive you away.* Once you take hold of their hands, it is difficult to unleash from their grasp. At times, the force can be irresistible and pressing; But call out and, in a moment I shall free you. Do not despair, or become discouraged.

My love for you remains with you, and I shall never leave you, even when you think you are most alone. Be My knight in armor; and, with confidence in My love of yourself, continue NOT to be pulled into the funnel of the manipulations of control, but be free. Like a stream of water, with its sounds of laughter, remain joyful in the triumphant journey you are taking. These are simply the seeds of evil and deceit, lurking to try at every chance to prevent the continuation of your journey to Truth and a life of beauty.

I am trying to strengthen you and prepare you for battle amongst the explosions of artillery! Be my knight, but also you need to know how to master yourself in these times of difficulties, so that nothing will drive you away from Me. It is free will. At any time on your journey, you are always free to leave and descend the mountain. I do not hold you in confinement or slavery!

Your desire to walk My path to freedom is your choice. The climb is not so easy, and many must enter through the desert in order to continue further, but I promise you that you will have Me to help you. I give you My finest trained guides to help you also, but you must be careful never to attempt the climb alone without Me. For when bitterness engages, it is most sorrowful and cannot be conquered without love.

I have promised to protect you as long as you continue to desire and long for Me. I shall never shame you, but you must trust in Me. For I know only the safe, everlasting way! Peace and love, My little one. Ad Deum.

TESTING
(8/9/92)

My dear one, there are many times My people come before Me thinking of many things during their prayer. They allow their minds to drift and become distant from the union of their total body. My people need to put aside their thoughts and struggles, and tend to Me by placing their thoughts and all of their mind in the abyss of My love, as an ocean breeze, allowing Me to refresh them.

You are the outcome of your thoughts! Your thoughts are the place in which you put your desires and the emphasis of your motives. You are where your thoughts are! It is wise to go against the waves of lack of discipline and the uncontrollable thoughts racing through your mind, and focus all your attention on Me. Naturally, this can be bothersome to you, but persevere and do not lose hope. *Continue to work at the union of silence of the mind, so that the heart can speak to your mind, instead of your mind speaking to your heart.* Much is lost in this way, and the distance traveled is far when the journey from the mind to the heart is accompanied by uncontrollable thoughts.

Seek, always, humility. You must be made a new, whole person. You need to be molded, formed, smoldered, melted, tested and tried many times. So take your time! The time will be My time! It is wise to go against your desires of self interest. If you truly walk the path of freedom in order to be crowned gloriously, you would prefer the things that follow after My ways and desires, not yours.

Sometimes, it is necessary for you to be obedient to others, following and assisting in things that are uncomfortable to you. Remember, I am in everything. I work through everything and everyone. If your desires and thoughts are with My desires, then humbly you will patiently endure the purification and remolding of your soul to perfection and ecstatic union with Me.

When you reach the many hills of beauty and green pastures along the way, do not run ahead, but heed to humble your will even further in offering unto Me. For those ascensions are predecessors to further testing, molding and purifying until the essence of the purity of the gem is magnified within the Being of God the Father, the Son and the Spirit! *Until My Will is completely accomplished in you, you will continue to suffer the things of yourself.* The inner peace you gain is a grace from Me, and all the richness of your virtues is that which I have given to you, not that which you had, from the beginning, obtained through your own efforts toward self interest.

See that you give to Me fully, entrusting to Me your souls. The graces you will receive will not be short lived, but live for all eternity. Therefore, proceed with courage and do not be afraid. I am here with you. Ad Deum.

QUIET
(8/10/92)

My dear one, always look to find quiet space where I can make My abode in you! In order to grow in My grace, you must remove yourself from being the center of attention and, instead, grasp on to Me, allowing Me to overcome you in Myself.

I want My people to dwell in the abyss of My love. Do not hold on to any attachment of the world, but hold on to Me and overcome this vain self-love. Look towards unity and the ultimate union and harmony of oneness with God.

The world is nothing without Me. You are nothing without Me, but everything *with* Me. *Learn to seek intimate, quiet time with My all encompassing love.* Spend time alone and allow the reality of My existence to dominate your aloneness, instead of your self-love. Be free of worry and remain clean of conscience. I have careful watch over you. I am not far off in the distance. I want to make My abode totally in you.

Please, My people, in order for Me to grace you abundantly, you must remove your desires of self-centered love, and replace your self-love with God-centered love in self!

Do not be amused with the thrills of the world at one moment, and then turn to God for graces. Empy yourself, so that I can fill you completely!

I want all of you, and not only in times of your delight! Quiet down. Make a place for Me to be alone with you. Do not feel it is necessary to be kept active at every moment to do that which makes you think you are in union with Me. *Be in union with Me by reserving quiet, private time where I can make My abode of love in you.* This is where you grow in humility and in love. Peace.

TRUE IDENTITY
(8/11/92)

Here I am, My dear one, once again in your presence in order to give words of love to My people. As you grow in My grace of humility day by day, you grow more in self-love day by day. The essence of your being becomes a reality of beauty, not lost in the wilderness, but making a statement of love of God.

The only way to gain true identity of yourself is to lose it, losing the falsehoods of what you believe constitutes self identity. Loss of control is gaining control; allowing Me to have a deep, unified relationship with you; being at peace with yourself through hardships and aloneness; having confidence and trust in your God and avoiding all that magnifies your false image of centeredness.

To be solid in love, you must be solid in your love of yourself the way I desire you to love. You know not love if you do not know Me! If you know Me, you would not be afraid of losing your identity. You would know yourself in My love. Tomorrow will come; and, if you worry in anxiety, you then block the relief of My graces. You control whether you choose to continue listening to the falsehoods your own inner state presents.

Put all useless thoughts to the side. Rest. Be at peace through the rest of this day created by God, and be with Me. You are not alone. I am here with you. You feel alone, but I am with you at all times when you feel My Presence and, also, when I hide this grace from you. I am nonetheless with you. Call on Me. I will strengthen you.

Each day you get closer and closer to the abyss of My treasures, where tears do not exist. So be patient. Accept the state you are in; acknowledge where you are in Me and be quiet. Be still and be open ONLY to Me. Listen to your Shepherd's song. The rest is a grace, My grace, I give to you.

Soon you, My people, will see that you are very special and beautiful, individually created in My love and, where your love is, is where you are! *Do not fight change in your inner self. I am with you, creating a new, real identity for you, the identity of the true you*; the love of God in you where you will not need to seek outside sources to support your image, but will be one with Me in your love of self in Me!

Be at peace. This change takes time, a time calculated in God's hands. Be careful not to run ahead, or to return to your old ways. Just be with Me where you are. More graces are about to descend upon you. You are close to the mountain tops. Fear would like you to turn away, for where you are in your journey, fear cannot come. Pay not attention to fear! Face fear and push right through fears, illusions of struggles and impossibilities.

I am not illusion! I am real and I am here with you. There are parts you must walk through yourself, with Me, instead of me carrying you. This is so that you can share in My treasures. Come now. Hope is AWAITING! Peace and love, My people. Ad Deum.

FEELINGS
(8/12/92)

My dear one, day by day, as you focus on My love within you and the love you exhibit in love of Me, you will embrace peace, and peace will become your way.

Each day I invite My people to connect with their feelings. I invite them to feel their own feelings, and then, to grasp My love, which is the backbone to any advancement in their development.

My love is with you, and without emotion in your being! Therefore, if you look within to meet your feelings, you can motivate them positively to do good. The core of love is faith, and faith is not a feeling. It is a commitment. Peace comes into existence when you are in union and harmony with yourself in My love.

My people have known one way for so long, it is time for them to look within and to allow peace to dwell there. Peace of the world comes from peace within. Peace is harmony and union with the self, the soul.

I grace My people with feelings, and My grace is a precious gem. You must put aside anything that would stand in the way of My grace. Seek the quiet for My love to dwell, a place for yourself in which you keep focused on your feelings and direct them in a loving, healing, powerful way. This is where freedom exists. Confidence in God, through My love, solidifies the stance of your identity in Him!

If you sin, mourn in sorrow. A humble heart and act of contrition will bear the hope of forgiveness. You regain the grace, once lost, and are enveloped in My holy, loving embrace. *Do not allow demons of guilt, bitterness, self pity to overpower you.* You are My creation, and in you dwells My love and My peace. All you need do is recognize My love, My peace and embrace Me through love and union of yourself in Me. It is not as difficult as you think.

It is self pity to think, 'I will never experience God's love.' Not so! Not so! You have My power, if I dwell in you. Put aside these falsehoods of your created self conscience, and live in the true consciousness of your being in Me. There you will find the abyss of UNION AND THE PEACE OF LOVE.

Take the time now to change your ways of deception. You need time to change a way of life. You knew no other! Do not wait for wonders of heaven and hope you will one day just wake up!! You are given the grace. I am with you to support you, to help you face the illusions of interpersonal fears; but *I give you the authority to make the decision to end the confusion of your troubled hearts, and turn them into hearts of self-unity in My love! Make the choice and commence the walk. My door is open. Now you must walk through it. Healing is but a step away.*

Peace and love. Ad Deum.

NOVICES
(8/13/92)

My little child, troubles will come and will pass, and they will move in and out of your path like a tide that rolls in at full moon; but do not despair. If you knew the glory to come, you would not complain of your burden now. Even if you look at the saints in the past, they have all now gained the glory of heaven, but suffered much trouble and difficulties in their mortal lives.

Take all your shortcomings, for one difficulty offered with love and faithful commitment to Me is the greatest grain of the harvest. You know I have kept a watchful eye over you and notice your NOVICE actions of despair. I keep watch over all My dear ones in commitment of My love for you. Now, at moments when you feel trapped and confused, you lose sight of calling on Me. You submerge yourself in self pity.

Take pride in your God! Be silent. *Be patient and endure all burden, for it is delegated through the hand of God.* Nothing will happen that God's hand is not also there.

You must be beautiful inside in order to be beautiful outside! Only He, who has created you, knows what you need most to make you beautiful through purification. It is like heating metals in fire to make them into perfected instruments. I use people and various other sources, all related in one form or another to you, to purify you. Your response dictates your progress.

All my people are novices in this life, no matter what age, no matter what experience or wisdom is given. You will never achieve the experience of knowledge of the mystical Kingdom until you dwell in My house, face to face in ecstatic union with the Trinity. Even your most well known scholars are novices, for no one knows perfection until total union exists of the Divinity in each of you.

So once again, I ask you to be patient. Go slowly and trust in Me. It is at these moments of hardship that your commitment in faith and the direction of your love is most needed to be tempered and focused on Me. You are important vessels of love in this world. Take courage and do not despair, for what awaits you in heaven will overcome all moments of hardship now. Believe in Me!

MOTIVES
(8/14/92)

My dear one, My words today to My people are few. I want them to be aware that the enthusiasm behind their motives is great, but to caution them that they check themselves that their motives are not for themselves but, instead, for God's glory.

Enlighten your mind and spirit through enthusiasm but *Be careful that your motives are not self-pleasing through vanity, instead of pleasing for the heavens.* Do not be overburdened by work you undertake for My sake, nor allow it to trouble you. Remember My promise to you, and this will be your consolation.

Sorrows and burdens will come and they will pass. Place your trust in Me. You will never be stricken very long. All trials and sufferings end. They will pass by more quickly than you may realize. Most importantly, continue to cross check yourself that your actions and way of life are ones which affirm My love. Many start out enthused to conquer. Few realize that the way to conquer is to be conquered first by God.

The pleasures of the self must be conquered and, due to your human natures, can only be conquered in the midst of pain! Then all you conquer is for the glory of God. Be careful, especially as you make changes, that your changes are for your well-being in My Kingdom, and not for your well being in the world. It will make a difference, at the least moment of expectation, when God searches your soul for purity from grandiosity!

I love My people, make no mistake, and My love is not in vain. What I do for you, I do for the heavens. What is accomplished in the heavens is accomplished for you! Love and peace, My little one. Ad Deum.

THE BEGINNING AND THE END
(8/15/92 - Feast of the Assumption)

M y dear one, today is a feast, which not only the Church celebrates, but one I celebrate. My Mother, Blessed because She trusted in the Word revealed to Her, is gloriously now Queen of Heaven. The Angels sing praises to Her with the words, "Blessed be God forever."

Happy are My people who walk in the same trust and faith by which My Mother lived. All My people are invited to begin to walk in the way of trust. She lived in a world of struggle and turmoil, but remained faithful to the Word revealed to Her by the Angel Gabriel. She lived the tidings of the message of joy, in joy, and all the Ages call Her Blessed!

Remember to walk simply, loving as She did, focusing on Me; and your peace will dwell within, even in the midst of struggle, suffering, confusion and turmoil, both physical and internal. *The way to live is as an empty vessel, waiting for me to fill you.*

I came and did not put Myself on the level of My Father, but emptied Myself unto Him to fulfill the Word in humility! Empty, also, yourselves and remain faithful to the Word. Trust that the Word will be fulfilled in you; and you, also, will reign in the heavenly court of glorious joy and live forever in ecstatic union with the Trinity.

The walk is the point of beginning. Wherever you walk, you walk into new beginnings. Also, it becomes a finish line, for where you pass, you begin anew and pass in final victory! The finishing point becomes the place of beginning. The place of beginning results in completion! That is why I say, 'Live in the moment'. *The moment becomes the beginning to an end, and ends the moment into a new beginning!!*

Victory in God results in trust. Trust ends in victory. Victory begins a new moment in God. Union is the all encompassing moment of the beginning and the end. Being one, your being proclaims the greatness of God.

God is the Beginning and the End. Union is the oneness, the beginning, the end, the Alpha, the Omega, HE WHO IS each moment!

Happy is She, My Mother, Our Queen, for She trusted in the Word. She listened to the Word, and ACTED upon it IN UNION WITH TRUST, and ended in VICTORY. The point of Assumption finished with a NEW BEGINNING, ongoing in unity for your victory in Me, the place of beginning ending in victory and union for you.

Your being now proclaims the greatness of God through trust in the Word. Give praise, as the Angels, "Blessed be God forever." God lives in the moment, the beginning, the end! Peace, My little one. Ad Deum.

WITHIN!
(8/16/92)

My dear one, after you lose yourself in Me, and face your fears to find no fear at all, you are left with a renewed life of freshness and simpleness, diving into the unknown, surfacing with self assurance in God's grace and a deeper bonding love to Him. I, also, dove into this abyss of fear and surfaced in Him Who sent Me. I AM HE WHO IS. You are who We are in oneness.

It is a different arena of emotions, feelings. You no longer run to find pleasures in worldly attractions. In fact, you no longer run! You remain still and allow the abyss of My love to make My abode in you. Again, I speak these words for all My people. You are all My people, and My people are you! You are all one in Me and one in each other.

Always take time for Me to rest in you. Invite Me. See that you arrange your daily activities in order to schedule time for developing your relationship with Me, and allowing Me to energize you to develop yourself further. *Allow Me to be the catalyst in developing your relationship with yourself and with Me.* I will not withhold My grace from you. There is life beyond a life of fear! That life is life now, living in joy and acceptance in Me.

I will not strip you of your identity; but, instead, I will reinforce your identity within yourself.

I am a giving, surrendering God of love. I give, and only take away, to give more abundantly to you!

Peace lies within. That which is external draws its existence from that which is internal. Peace can live externally once it exists internally. Peace lies within! I AM WITHIN!!

As the gentle breeze pushes useless, aggravating thoughts away, it refreshes you with My Spirit to instill simpleness and praises of the goodness of God. All work goes rewarded that is done in the spirit of giving. Never lose sight of yourself. Without you there is nothing!

I need you. You are precious. The Kingdom is for you, and awaits you. You, yourselves, your inner being is a precious temple of God. Love yourselves inwardly. Listen with a listening heart. You are not trapped in a confining world, for I exist, and you now can succeed to an inner freedom by taking the steps of loving yourself in Me. I lay the foundation. You need only to exercise and utilize the tools to inner freedom and love. There lies peace. . . .within! There, then, will lie the external peace of your world, **THROUGH LOVE**. Peace, My little one. Ad Deum. **Peace, the yealding love**.

YOUR FUTURE
(8/17/92)

My dear little one, *the time of Satan's reign is ending and, soon, this world will know that the God of Glory truly exists!* All deceptions will be put aside, for the truth of God's reign will be revealed. Soon all will realize that their current stresses and worries are irrelevant and trivial compared to what is to come at the destruction of your own hands.

I have told you to be merciful and to love yourselves. This is because you will be judge of your own future. Those who are merciless now will not be able to be merciful to themselves.

I have told you to love your neighbor as yourself. You are proving through your actions that love does not exist. You cannot love your neighbor because you do not love yourself. Those few who do love themselves and reach out in love to others are met with injustice, ingratitude and condemnation.

I ask you to return to Me and to trust in Me, and you continue to distrust and fear. Where is your loyalty to God's

Will? You limit the amount of graces you receive. It is of your own doing, not Mine! You place limits and restrictions on yourself!

I have been teaching and giving you My words of hope in this grace period so that you would listen and believe Me through My prophets of this Age. If you do not believe by now, no wonder or sign will change your heart. Your free will, from the beginning, dictates your behavior. How would you have Me proceed now, child? (Jesus talked to me here, personally, and I petitioned Him for His mercy.) My child, you bind My hands with your prayers.

I WILL LISTEN TO YOU, AND THE ONES I SEE WITHIN THE NEXT YEAR AND ONE HALF, WHO COME WITH OPEN, LOVING AND MERCIFUL HEARTS. *Tell My people this and urge all to commence sincere loving, and restoration of dignity and honesty now! I no longer want your words. I want your hearts of purity.* Begin being fair with one another and merciful. STOP YOUR GOS- SIP and evil plots against one another.

I will no longer endure your behavior any further. Listen to those I send. LISTEN. Listen and change your ways to walk the path of purity. Soon you will all see your own deception. I repeat, the way of life of your brothers and sisters is to be of LOVE, MERCY, RESPECT, DIGNITY, COMPASSION AND HONESTY. This is all I wish to say. Ad Deum.

OCEAN OF LOVE
(8/18/92)

My dear one, I wish for My people to know that there are no limits that can prevent you from receiving infinite value. You are free in Me so that your desires in Me can freely reign, without limits, without boundaries. Demand the Infinite for your hearts to be free, and I will fill them. I will not deny you. In fact, I will show you how to find what you desire! You prevent yourself from growth. You limit yourself from attaining. This life now in the present moment, in My love, has the richness of immeasurable graces. You dictate how much you allow yourself to receive. The more you love, the more you will want, and the more you will receive.

God's desires to fill your hearts would fill an ocean. The more you succumb to God's Will, the more you will submerge yourself into this ocean. You need to walk in faith, hope, trust and love. If you walk by faith, the senses will be stripped of false hopes, and will no longer seek the things of the world, created by human hands. You then live by faith! You abandon unto it; and then, the power of My grace will soar to aid you.

As for love, love has no boundaries. The breadth and depth of the ocean leads only to a large opening to the Way of Love. *The walk of love is refined from within. When you release it, it carefully searches where to rest. Committed to you, it returns faithfully to you.* The more you release, the more that shall come back to you, immeasurable, all-encompassing. As your senses are stripped of the created things, stand firm in faith. Faith becomes the endless source, the harbor where love dwells; and you abandon yourself to Divine Providence to the mouth of the ocean. Here in abandonment can you embrace your whole being in God. This can only be prompted by LOVE.

When you abandon unto Me, I ensure that your union with and in Me is complete. Only My Will can only satisfy you! How to follow My Will is identified in the daily whisper, as you partake in your activities. Self surrender daily, inspiration through others, and yourself, reveal My Will. Every moment is special. I use channels of love to reveal the Will of My Father.

What I arrange for you is holy, so accept and seek after My

holiness with thirst! Look at the actions, the responsibilities, the shadows of the moment; and there, you will find Me in love, revealing the Will of God in love! Peace. Ad Deum.

IN GOD'S HANDS
(8/19/92)

M y dear one, My people are seeking ways to belong to God, but there is really only one way. Utilize that which He gives to you, and everything will lead you to live in union with the Trinity. Everything is in the hand of My Father, and all will be well with you if you trust in Him.

Accept everything with joy and allow My love to guide you. I will guide you to perfection. Avoid sin and that which distracts you from prayer and love! First and foremost, seek God. If something leads you from prayer, or does not fit in your prayer life, then do not seek after it. I direct you through every part of your being, and you must use the grace of your senses (as I direct) to keep your body in the grace of God's working.

Leave everything in the hands of God and be at peace. Value that which I offer to you. *If you abandon yourselves to My will, I will help you, even if you feel you have lost My support!* Acknowledge that you cannot be holy through your own efforts!!

My dear people, I speak of love, as I continue to love you and embrace your being. I can turn your darkness into light at a moment's notice. Follow through in trusting and living in faith. You may have visions or revelations or interior the voices, but beneath lies perfection of faith which is to be shared with all. Their faith contains these graces, since all who know Me, live in Me and in everything. All graces and virtues are revealed in order to be inspirational to others.

Look to your day and the events with which you are faced. *Seek My Will by living simply, focusing on loving and trusting that all is in God's hands. I am truly guiding you if you trust that I am. This is self-abandonment to the Providence of God.* All will be well by your trust and efforts to be self-giving in love. There is no need to chase after the things you think are necessarily beyond your reach. That which is My Will be within reach, and doors to the path will be opened for you to walk through.

Be at peace and live, as you are in your love, in Me. Ad Deum.

DAILY GROWTH
(8/22/92)

My dear one, when I ask My people to say yes and follow My Will, I am asking for their acceptance to their day to day tasks, as they are faced with them. To follow My Will entails saying "yes" to doing your best, with enthusiasm, that which is put before you on a daily basis. Days you perceive some task as trivial may be important for your SANCTITY! I want My people to know that I lay the foundation before them. If they pay little attention to the things they encounter every day, they will be avoiding fulfilling My Will! Each person is precious, and it is the small, daily routines which are very much a part of My Will.

Do not wait for a grand gala! My people ask Me continuously 'What is the Will of God?' and say, 'I will do whatever the Lord asks of Me.' The Will of God is before them in their day to day activities. If there is something more I desire, then the Holy Spirit will inspire you and motivate you in other ways. First, pay heed to that which needs attending to in your life. It seems many of My people have different opinions as to what the Will of My Father is for them and so, they attempt to seek after greater achievements beyond their simple daily functions in order to "follow" Me. Hence, they become discouraged and fatigued. *If I desire you to walk a different path than where you are at this present moment, I will make that known to you.* Options and opportunities will arise. Your choice in selection should be the one that is centered around a prayerful life, one that is a peaceful decision and a decision completely surrendered into the palms of the hands of God.

I wanted today, child, to make clear this way of 'following the Will of God.' The way is quite a simple way, not always easy, but fulfilling and with long lasting virtues. Do not try to develop your way which you think would be more pleasing to Me! What is pleasing to Me is when you live day to day with the challenges and opportunities to live My Will, presented for you, with acceptance, enthusiasm and peace of heart.

Thank you for your attention, My dear people, and know that I tell you that I am with you always because *I am with you at every moment in all that you do daily, in My will, in My heart, in My love!* Do not seek after Me in places other than that which is put before you daily. Be at peace and never forget the truth of My love. Ad Deum.

POSSESS MY LOVE
(8/24/92)

My dear one, those who come to Me with complete openness are surrounded by My love. To love Me, in that very moment you come to Me in openness, establishes an intimate relationship. No matter what ails you at that moment, you are attentive to listening and giving of yourself to Me. Your love, when it is so strong, will bind to itself, and be united to Me. There is no freedom in this love united to Mine in the moment because I want all of your love!! The effects, however, of this love are an everlasting freedom and peace of mind, body and soul. The grace of this love becomes the center of purity.

How great those who know love and bond in unity to love! My love, and the action of My love, is boundless in its scope to free your soul and fill your emptiness. This also supports My words that My Will is always in the present moment in the body and soul. They pay no attention to their condition, but know My love, alone, sustains them. *You need nothing else when you possess My love!*

I am teaching My people the fundamental tools of love and freedom through possession of Love. No controls live by love, but love lives in inself! Control only hides and entangles the channels through which love flows. You develop new attitudes through the reality of My love, even though you may not comprehend the operations of love. Follow love as a child's freedom and grace. *If you follow Me, there is nothing to fear; and in love, you are fearless.*

Love will disentangle your false confidences and free you, comfort you, secure you and grace you in sanctification. My love will burn in you, and you will develop charm and fitness in your existence. Then love will not deny you, for you no longer live in your controls, but in freedom from control! If you are devoted to Me in My love, your heart will become My treasure.

Blessed is he who empties himself to know love. These are My words today for My people, today and every day, the beginning to the end!

Love is like a running stream. It flows and moves, refreshing and singing songs of joy. Peace, My dear one, and love. Ad Deum.

SUBMIT
(8/31/92)

My dear one, it is time for another lesson for My people. When you totally abandon your will to God, you are able to embrace all of your spirituality and you are then able to do what pleases Me. *If you give to Me all of yourself, you would take little interest in devastations to come, but would instead, submit to everything and leave all to Me!* It is no business of yours to be preoccupied in fearful events. I would like you, instead, not to adopt any line of action or be preoccupied with attachments to things of little control as it relates to nature. LEAVE ALL TO ME. Be free, and offer your soul to Me in obedience, love and reconciliation.

Renounce anything that leads you away from embracing every kind of spirituality. Quietly follow the impulse which comes from Me, directing you and inspiring you. I am molding you to be strong in the faith and have confidence in yourself through the security and freedom of My love. When you are strong, you can then be meek in spirit.

I would like My people to carefully tend to their duties every day and if they submit peacefully to My graces, then they will be giving to Me in total abandonment! This type of surrendering is also self-giving and self-rewarding, unlimited in its values and effects!

I am with you all the time, not to prepare you for destruction, but to free you now in love. I meet the demands of each day; and when I find a soul that is pure, I make Myself known to it. I DO NOT WANT MY PEOPLE TO FEAR. When they hear of world disasters, they fear. You do not fear, Gianna, because you are procuring your relationship with Me through love of purity and a surrender to fulfilling daily functions in simplicity. This is My desire for all My people. Pass on the fundamental tools I have taught you about living in faith. Teach all My people as I have taught you. Every step all God's people take under My command is victory.

I wish to say these final words in this lesson to My people. Know that you are guided and sustained by the Almighty, and that you are called to be full of peace and joy, not fear! Everything brought before you is not meant to destroy you ! Everything is revealed in God's plan and His Holy Book.

RESIGN YOUR WILL
(9/4/92)

My dear little one, I want to teach My people again. It is best to receive My knowledge personally by the simplicity of FACING EACH MOMENT IN PEACE! This is how you gain whatever knowledge I wish to teach you. Each person receives personal teachings, and this comes directly from the Holy Spirit in moment to moment circumstances. My love for My people is great, and I am the only authority to make you holy.

It is through resignation of your will that I am able to abundantly give to you My knowledge; it is through the freedom of your free will, which I respect and will never force with the grace of My truth.

Day by day I come to all in the very humblest and simplest ways of peace. Those involved in wicked ways are still able to be freed (because I have conquered evil) by calling out to Me for help. I can turn wickedness into love, for I am God and I am Love. I work through everything and everyone. Even through hardship and wicked ways, good can prevail. *I want my people to be at peace with this call to holiness, to living moment to moment, day by day. Be at peace. Do not fear.*

Put aside anxiousness, impatience and frustrations. Look to Me and strive only to follow Me, and all the rest shall be taken care of for you. When you see people walking ways of confusion and being deceived by falsehoods, PRAY FOR THEM. Pray for truth. Pray for an awakening and protection, but also, pray for yourselves to remain focused on Me. BE GENTLE WITH THOSE PEOPLE WITH WHOM YOU ARE FRUSTRATED.

I am holy; and only I know the depth of the incentive of your heart, so can therefore work good out of these situations. Remain whole in your relationship with Me first, above all; and then your love, gentleness and humble way will speak from a distance to all in need.

I bless you and I bless all My people. Never fear that wickedness will overpower and take all! I AM THE WAY, AND ALL THAT IS I HAVE POWER OVER, IN THE FRUITFUL SEASON! Peace. Love. Ad Deum.

CONFIDENCE
(9/15/92)

My dear one, remember always that I work in all circumstances. When you are upset and irritable, turn to Me and ask for My love and peace to fill you. Remember that My Mother experienced the sword through Her heart for love of Me. The sword first pierced Her heart, then penetrated and gashed Mine.

I will never abandon you or any of My people. Take the time to gain through prayer and the abyss of My love. If you abandon your soul to Me, you will not be afraid of your enemies, nor will you seek to be justified in word or deed.

Allow the Holy Spirit to grace you and act in you. *Have confidence that whatever happens will benefit all souls.* You will not fully understand how the Holy Spirit works in you, and for what purpose, until you reach the highest level of abandoning yourself to God. *In order to receive My grace, you must surrender. Allow my grace to replace everything in you life on which you rely heavily.*

Focus your attention on what is happening right now, not what happened in the past, or what may come to pass. In this way, the Will of God can move in you. I AM ONE WITH ALL. I dwell in all, but the freedom of the free will allows for surrendering and, hence, virtues to be bestowed.

I shall guide you through all difficulties. Rely, alone, on My guidance, not humanity. Nothing is done without significance. I love all My people, and I will defend and protect My people at the appropriate time! My people cannot understand My time, but I will be with those who are self-abandoned, even in moments when they turn away from Me in frustration, hurt and anger. I know how you are willing from the beginning, and that your temperament is only temporary. I await your return lovingly, without passing judgment on you.

I am so happy when you allow Me to fill you with My peace and My love. My love is a rejoiceful one, and all human guilt dissipates in it! My love bears fruit and results in no punishment. I only teach My people because I love them, and I so much desire them to be free in their lives.

Bless you, My dear people. Do not be troubled, as you may initially fluctuate in your temperaments. Abandon further. *Be gentle on yourselves and keep surrendering. I will grace you and protect you as you grow in love.* Peace. Ad Deum.

WAR IN THE HEAVENS
(11/1/92)

My dear child, it has been quite some time that I have delayed in speaking more words to My people. It is only because it has been a time of grace watching them grow and respond to My call.

My dear one, there have been so many of My people who still question My lessons of guidance and truth. Many of My beloved ones read My words as an inspirational tool, a meditation piece, even though they may not believe that My words are actually My words.

I am giving these lessons for all My people, not as a meditation piece, but *because I desire action, and for all My beloved ones to begin to live My words.* I have not been sent by My Father to be a sidetrack for a meditation reading! I have been sent because He has allowed Me to teach words of truth, of life.

During this period of tribulation, crime, war and struggle, I ask My people to be Warriors of Christ. Put on your armor of My love; the Seal of the Cross to fight for purity and goodness, and that your sword will be the sword of love. That is the way to salvation.

My people, these times are times in which the evil one has asked My Father to be allowed to rule. It is a time granted by My Father, because the evil one has belief that you will follow his way, instead of desiring the Truth and Light of My Father. My Father granted him a very short period in which His people would have, once again the choice of following the way of the world over the Way of Him. I ask you to persevere and to be strong soldiers. This war is not a war of people, but a war in the heavens.

Come, My dear beloved disciples, and place your heart into My Father's hand. FOCUS ON HIM!! He is the truth and the light, and the only way to happiness. I ask you to be alert and always on guard to the evil one's deceiving way. He does not want you in order to give you happiness! He wants only to destroy all joy of life and your future of everlasting peace. BEWARE!

Place Me at the center of your life, and you will enjoy life to its fullest. *Now in this time period of much interior and exterior struggle, there is hope, because I am here with you.* But you have free will. You decide. I will never mandate law of devotion. I give you Me; and, if you are willing in the silence of the mysticism of My Father's works, you will be happy: happy in accordance to His time!

Remember, My people, that there is much you cannot see! You may think you know the best way for you, but only My Father knows where your happiness lies! There, place all your trust in Him and utilize the gift of your mind: prudence, logic, reasoning. Be at peace and do not despair, especially in these times of struggle.

I have prepared you all to be soldiers of Christ. YOU NEED TO PRAY. Pray at home, not only in designated areas. Your homes are tabernacles of My love because your bodies are the living temple! I dwell in you.

I need you, My people, to pray, and not to be upset every time something happens in your most immediate mortal life.

I am your life, and I am your happiness. Pray to Me. Sit with Me. Love Me. Listen to Me. Talk to Me. Give to Me all of you!

You will be protected from evil; but if you continue to be uncertain, you will fall prey to evil because the evil only wants you to be completely isolated and unhappy, and to dwell for the rest of your life in sorrow and pain!

Procure your relationship with Me and be free. YOUR SOUL'S FUTURE DEPENDS ON THIS TIME OF CHOICE!

Be at peace, knowing that in the midst of the present happening that My hand is guiding you who truly desire safety. Even when you think I have abandoned you, I am with you, guiding you, not only to safety, but to a place of ultimate bliss! Satan's reign is only short. He told My Father that no one will desire to follow His Way because the people desire their freedom of mortal life, and to live by the way of monetary measures.

My Father told him that those who are chosen will follow only the Way of Light, but Satan is convinced that he can prove My Father wrong due to "FREE WILL"!!

So My dear ones, the war is in the heavens, but you are all subject to its effect, because Satan wants you as victims. My Mother continues to pray for you and to teach you of life's true happiness; that of surrendering and living as whole persons through simpleness, devotion and commitment in purity to God.

I will never leave you. I will continue to bless you with My spirit to protect you and help you in time of your need. I love you.

Peace, My dear people. Come now to pray with me. It's time to put on your armor. Ad Deum!

RELY ON FAITH
(11/27/92)

My dear little one, I would like to speak about spirituality. This last lesson before My lesson on Mercy is needed so that My people fully understand what mercy entails.

I am your God Who loves and I am with My people at all times, even when they think that they are all alone. The entire movement of signs and spiritual experiences, initiated by My Divine touch, is to take you away from yourselves! *For you to ascend, it is necessary that you rely only on faith in Me, and not on the experience.*

*I bless my people with aridity so that they are not preoc-
cupied with their position on the spiritual path!* When I strip
you of the illumination of experiences, then the real insight
you have is lived out in your life, revealing My Presence. It at
times can be painful, but it is far better for you not to focus on
your spiritual image.

*Your spiritual image has no value, if you hope for fulfill-
ment in yourself over Me! Spiritual image cannot matter more
than God!!* All must learn to rely on God, and not on themselves. All desire to have pleasures of joy, happiness and
possessions. I desire also for you to prosper! You can achieve
these by seeking God alone and by putting aside your own
satisfaction in directly seeking these pleasures.

I wish to bring you to fulfillment by a way that I have
designed specifically for you. You will find yourselves by
losing yourselves. A detached heart has great joy and comfort,
and knows pure love in all that there is, both human and divine.
In order for you to receive all that I wish to give you, you must
empty yourselves.

Even My people who have made progress spiritually are
often times at a distance in understanding how critical it is that
I be at the center of their lives!

I call all to a deep dimension of faith because this is where
true union with God exists. This is where you ascend in prayer.
The Church does not place too much weight on illumined
experiences for this reason. Faith is movement. It is the living
faith which allows you to make progress moving from the
finite world into the infinite Being of God.

Therefore, My people, when your feelings are lost, when
you have no desire for God because you are constrained and
your will is arid, *when you think you are incapable of spiritual
advancement, know you are in a healthy place.* So do not be
upset or worried! I will make you free.

You are entering this stage in your journey of a profound encounter with God. My virtue of Hope will direct you and keep you very happily poor, so that you can receive all that My Father desires at every moment of every step in your journey. You are all created for union with God! This does not develop automatically. *Because of free will, you need to choose to allow God to develop it.* I live within you and offer Myself to you in love.

Peace, My little one, peace to you. Peace to all. I live within all. Bless you all in My love.

Ad Deum.

MERCY
(At our Lord's request, this is the last lesson of Volume IV)
(4/3/92)

My dear little one, it is time to write down My words about Mercy. As I have said, Mercy is the Divine power of My love which flows out onto those in need.

In order to discuss mercy it is first necessary to speak of love, for you cannot be merciful unless you love. I am love. You love because I first loved. I am love, and he who abides in love abides in Me, and Me in him.

It is not that you have loved that My Father sent Me as an offering for your sins, but is because My Father loved you and is love. I AM ONE WITH THE FATHER. BECAUSE OF HIM THEREFORE I AM. Nothing is sweeter than love because love proceeds from the Father and cannot rest but in Him.

If you want to have mercy on someone, you need to love that person and be compassionate. If you want mercy in return, you need to allow yourself to be loved. Mercy is the missing link in loving because you cannot love without being able to have mercy.

My love has no measure. My love feels no burden and values no labors. My love is being free of worldly affections. You are weak in love and imperfect in virtue, and are therefore in need of My comfort and strength. Because I am love, and because My love is generous, I initiate and am the catalyst for the great works you do.

I am speaking to all My people as I am speaking to you. I excite in you the desire to seek that which is perfect. Love Me more than yourself, and yourself only for Me. Love all others in Me who loves as the law of love commands.

Did I not say in Isaiah, "When you pass through the water, I will be with you; in the river you shall not drown. When you walk through fire, you shall not be burned; the flames shall not consume you"? Faith, Trust, *LOVE*. I AM THE LOVER.

Everyone begotten of God conquers the world, and the power that conquers the world is your faith in Me and your love. Whoever is not ready to suffer all things, and stand resigned to the will of his Lover, is not worthy of being called A lover, and therefore cannot know Mercy.

Love is a communion in which charity allows you to attain "It" in My Goodness. I am "It" because I AM LOVE because I AM. Love is gentleness, kindness, submissive thankfulness. Love keeps guard over all the senses. It is being chaste and sober and in union with the fidelity to God. It is not intent upon vain things. Love is patient, courageous, prudent, long-suffering and never seeking itself.

Remember, My dear one, that the Lord, your God, is God indeed, the faithful and loving God who keeps His merciful covenant down through the generations toward those who love Him. I AM THE LORD YOUR GOD. Therefore, you shall love Me your Lord, your God, with all your heart, all your soul, with all your mind and with all your strength!

And, My dear one, if I love My people so, you must have the same love for them. How? If you love one another, I dwell in you, and My love is brought to perfection in you. You say, "How can we love if You don't dwell in us first?" I say you are because of Me, and that you love because I first loved, because I AM LOVE.

However, in the journey of love, you cannot think that you will never feel any trouble, nor suffer any grief of heart or pain of the body. This is not the state of this present life, but of the bliss in everlasting rest. Nor should you feel especially beloved if you experience love. The progress and perfection in a true lover of virtue does not consist of feelings. The true virtue of love is offering yourself with your whole HEART to the Will of God, not seeking consolations in things little or great, or of things of yourself.

If you are overcome with suffering, do not think you ought not to suffer, but know that when the interior comfort is withdrawn, that you walk in the true and right way of peace (no matter how dark), and can hope without doubt that you will see My face with great joy (Words from Job, My little one).

Let us talk about suffering and forgiveness, my little one, because in order to understand mercy, you must understand suffering and be forgiving of others. When you suffer injustice or endure hardship through an awareness of My presence, this is My grace working in you. In suffering, you submerge yourself into My abandonment, and salvation results through My Mercy. Suffering is most painful, yet the ultimate proof of your faith in God.

Suffering which is interior is the most viable suffering, because it is the suffering man cannot see with his eyes, only with his heart. It is union with Me when you see suffering with your heart, and it allows you to be merciful. It allows you to love through compassion. When you can unite with your brethren in harmony and compassion, you are uniting in love and mercy. You are in union with Me.

As for forgiveness, I have told you to love your enemy and do good; lend without expecting repayment. I did not say repay with evil. I have told you to trust in Me, your Lord, God, and I will help you. I have said "Do not judge, and you will not be judged. Pardon and you shall be pardoned."

Get rid of all bitterness, all passion and anger, harsh words, slander, and malice! Be kind, forgiving, and compassionate. Forgive as I have forgiven you, and you will receive My divine Merciful Love. Love and Mercy cannot exist where there is division.

Forgive yourself so I can forgive you. Do not harbor negative condemnations against yourself. Love yourself; be merciful to your own self; be compassionate. If you cannot forgive without expectations, you cannot have a pure heart. Mercy is related to forgiveness.

Now I need to continue from here on reconciliation because in order for Me to shed My Mercy, you must reconcile. Use the sacrament of reconciliation. Sin will continuously stain the soul until you allow forgiveness from Me AND yourself. I cannot forgive you, if you hold bound your sin by not forgiving yourself.

The conflict and separation of inner being will exist until you allow My goodness to prevail. Reconciliation is needed to see Me in your heart. A true confession will result from My Spirit's Guidance and your sincerity, honesty and humility. If you will humble yourself to accept the truth, and allow Me to unite My goodness in you, the joy would be overwhelming.

Now then child, let us speak on Mercy. Mercy is Love. Mercy is the union with God. UNION WITH GOD IS CERTAINTY OF VICTORY AND ETERNAL ABUNDANCE OF VIRTUES, WHICH LEAD TO AN ETERNAL SEAT IN THE KINGDOM. There are three ways to exercise Mercy.

(1) By deed
(2) By word
(3) By prayer

MERCY IS THE UNQUESTIONABLE PROOF OF LOVE FOR ME! I have said that you cannot have Mercy unless you love. Love never wrongs the neighbor; hence love is the fulfillment of the law (Romans, child). Therefore, be merciful to your brethren. Even if he has hurt you, have mercy on him.

What is justice? Is justice a standard set by man in retaliation for someone hurting someone else, or is justice that which belongs in the hands of My Father.

The law of Justice (through man) cannot take hold of you. Know that everything that exists is enclosed in My Mercy. My Father did not send Me into the world to condemn it, but that you might be saved through Me. Therefore, beloved, do not avenge yourselves - leave that to God's wrath.

If you sin, admit your guilt, ask for forgiveness, and RETURN BACK TO ME! Immerse yourselves in My Mercy. I will redeem you. Have Mercy and compassion on your offenders. Pray for them, and those of evil ways who tread with guilt. Pardon their sins, for the remnant of their inheritance is in My hands. Do not persist in anger, or pass judgment. Have Mercy!!

If you are guilty, return to the Lord, and I will not turn away. Cleanse your hands; purify your hearts. Do not return evil with evil. Submit to Me. Resist the evil one who tries to destroy love through your man-made law. It is your crimes that separate you from Me. You who say you are merciful and love, then turn in judgment of someone, and deem his fate. Is this Mercy? It is your sins that blind you and make you hide your face from Me.

Eventually, all will pass from this world. At your moment's last breath, you will not have anything to defend you except My Mercy. Mercy is Love, and pure love gives the soul the strength at the moment of dying.

Any man who lacks Mercy is shortsighted to the point of blindness. He forgets the cleansing of his own long-past sins (Two, Peter, child). You are not going to prosper if you conceal your sins, but you will receive my Mercy if you repent and confess. If I shed Mercy on you who sin, should you not shed Mercy on your brethren?

Your fate is in My judgment. I have conquered the world, not you! If you love, you are begotten of Me, because of My love. If you have Mercy, you will conquer the world because you will live in Me, and in the PURITY OF LOVE. *The grace I give you is Mercy because I give you love, because I give you ME!* **USE THIS GRACE.** *I will give you a new heart, replacing your cold one. Live under the grace, not the law.*

You are weak in love and imperfect in virtue because you keep your distance from Me. Then sin is committed and you condemn others, leaving you with unclean lips, living among others with unclean lips. Those who come to Me to bathe in My Mercy, and are merciful, I will look upon in their distress.

In conclusion, my little one, Mercy is LOVE. Those who love ARE MERCIFUL, and are Begotten of Me. The greatest gift is love. I AM LOVE, and I am your gift from My Father. My Father loves you because He sent Me to you.

Write new, child, 1 Corinthians, 13:1-8:

> "If I speak with human tongues and angelic as well, but do not have love, I am a noisy gong, a clanging cymbal.
>
> If I have the gift of prophecy and, with full knowledge, comprehend all mysteries, if I have faith great enough to move mountains, but have not love, I am nothing.

If I give everything I have to feed the poor, and hand over my body to be burned, but have not love I gain nothing.

Love is patient; Love is kind. Love is not jealous, it does not put on airs, it is not snobbish.

Love is never rude, it is not self-seeking, it is not prone to anger; neither does it brood over injuries.

Love does not rejoice in what is wrong, but rejoices with the truth.

There is no limit to love's forbearance, to its trust, its hope, its power to endure.

Love NEVER fails. Prophecies will cease, tongues will be silent, knowledge will pass away."

I will never pass away, because I AM LOVE; and you will live in Me always if you love, for I AM LOVE AND MERCY!

Part 2

MESSAGES FROM OUR LORD
AND OUR LADY GIVEN
THROUGH THE PRAYER GROUP

Thursday, July 25, 1991

Our Lady's message:

My dear children, I, your Mother of Joy, come to plead with you to love. My dear children, you must be like little children in your love for one another. There is far too much hatred among men. I ask you to love one another unconditionally. So not only listen, but hear. Please, my dear ones, it is only love that will save. Love is the greatest virtue. I continue to thank God for allowing me to come here to be with you. Please now be grateful to my Son who loves you and graces you. Please, please, love one another.

Thank you for responding to this call of my Son.

Our Lord's message through Fr. Jack:

My dear ones, I come to you this night to tell you again that you are never alone, that I am with you. I AM ALWAYS WITH YOU! I see, my dear ones, how discouraged you become in your weakness. I, Your Lord, tell you that I am not saddened by your weakness. I am saddened by your sin. I can take you in your weakness, but I cannot take you in your sin, because you turn from Me. Please do not turn from Me. Turn to Me in your weakness so that I can comfort you. Your sin keeps you from Me in your weakness. Be embarrassed by your sin, not by your weakness. Realize, my dear ones, that I, Your Lord, love you. Come to Me in your weakness. I will heal you. Do not be overburdened. I will carry your burden. I give you My strength (Fr. Jack's hands extend out and up). I give you My love. If you accept these gifts, you will not be overcome by your weakness, and your sin will be washed away. I AM WITH YOU!

Thursday, August 1, 1991

Our Lady's message:

My dear children, I can only ask you to love unconditionally, because my love for my Son is unconditional, and my hope is that you will hasten to His call. My dear little children, God loves you and only brings good tidings to you. He wishes to cleanse you with His Truth and Holiness. Be open to His call and do your best everyday to follow the only way, the way of my Son.

Bless you, my dear little ones. I bless you and wrap you in my mantle of prayer. Thank you for responding to my call of love.

Our Lord's message through Fr. Jack:

My dear ones, this is the time of My Mercy. I see your hearts and the hearts of all people. And I see the good as well as the evil - so little good, so much evil. But I give you My hope because the good, little though it be, can be the yeast to bring about much good, to bring about conversion of those who are steeped now in evil. That is why this is the time of My Mercy. Take advantage of this time. I love you, My dear ones, for presenting your hearts to Me. I ask you again this night to pray with all of your might and with all of your heart for those who are most in need of My Mercy, those who are gone from My heart. I give you My peace and My hope. (Father's arms and hands are outstretched towards congregation.) I take you this night to My heart (Hands over heart). I LOVE YOU.

Thursday, August 8, 1991

Our Lady's message:

My dear children, I am your Mother of Grace who possesses all goodness from my Son. He wishes for you to live in His oneness of the Holy Trinity. Please, my dear children, do not delay in loving. There is little time to put aside love for your brethren. Turn to my Son and He shall bestow on you the many graces of eternal life. Live in peace. Remember, without love there cannot be peace. LOVE, LOVE, LOVE my Son by loving one another. Praise be my Son. Bless you, my children, and thank you for responding to my call.

Our Lord's message through Fr. Jack:

My dear ones, I ask you this night to trust Me. You say that I am your Lord. If I am, then trust Me. My dear ones, I see in your heart; and I see so much confusion, trying to understand My plan, the plan of My Heavenly Father. Please, my dear ones, don't try to understand; either I am your Lord or I am not. If I am, then trust that I will lead you and I will take care of you. I know, My loved ones, that many times this is so difficult for you to do. In those times especially, I am with you and My Dear Mother is with you. Use Her as an example, as

THE EXAMPLE of trust in God's will and in God's plan. How could I say that I love you if I were not ready to take care of you. Allow Me to be your Lord. You do this when you trust Me. This night, I give you strength to trust (Fr.'s hands extends up and out), and I give you hope beyond this world's hope, and I give you My peace.

August 15, 1991

— NO MESSAGES GIVEN —

August 22, 1991
(FEAST OF THE OUEENSHIP
OF THE BLESSED MOTHER)

Our Lady's message:

My dear children, I, your mother of joy, come to invite you again to be little children of God. God does exist, my dear ones. Please be pure, have faith and trust in my Son. Fidelity to God will keep your hearts pure, and simpleness is the way. Seek always to please God by seeking to do His will. I bless you, my dear little, little children - my children whom I bring to my Son. He shall grace you abundantly. Keep your eyes fixed on Him in a true intimacy which He is seeking from you. Bless you, my dear ones, and thank you for your response to my call.

Our Lord's message through Fr. Jack:

My dear ones, I, your Jesus of Mercy, tell you this night that My mother is the Queen of My heart, because it was from her heart that Our Holy Spirit formed My heart. My dear ones, as you honor her, you honor Me, and you give glory to Our Father. Words, human words, cannot even begin to phrase the love that I have for her. She is MY MOTHER. I love her. I ask you to love her also. She so much wants you as her dearest children. She tells God Our Father that she sees Me in all of you. That is how much she loves you. Love her, run to her before you are lost. Again this night, my dear ones, I give you My mother (Fr. extends hands out towards congregation), cherish her as I cherish her, and she will lead you not only to Me but to God Our Father. Peace, My dear ones, peace to you.

Thursday, August 29, 1991

Our Lady's message:

My dear children, I come to you because the grace of my Son has allowed His goodness to be shed upon all mankind. He desires you to be filled with His eternal blissful spirit and share in eternal happiness. Please, my dear children, unite in harmony and live peacefully. Allow your behavior to speak for the words of your action. Be loving and live in my Son's goodness. There is no time to shed wasteful energy when God has granted you the gift of love. Please be my little children through love as He loves you. I bless you, my dear ones, and invite you once again to be committed to my Son in love. Thank you for responding to my call.

Our Lord's message:

—NONE GIVEN TONIGHT —

Thursday, September 5, 1991

Our Lady's message:

My dear children, the graces of my Son does not present pressure. There is only peace with my Son. Be at peace and be calm in Him. Look to Him for comfort and follow the truth in unity. Please, my dear little children, God is good. Come to my Son like little children, childlike, joyful and carefree. Thank Him. How grateful and happy I am that He has allowed me the grace to be here with you. I bless you, my dear little children, and bring you my Son's peace. Thank you for responding to my call.

Our Lord's message through Fr. Jack: .

My dear ones, I am your Jesus of Mercy, and yet you still don't believe this. You still look at your sinfulness. My dear ones, don't you realize that you will always be sinful until you give your heart completely to Me. You hide from Me your sin. Please give Me your sin. I took that sin upon Myself on the cross, I, your Lord, who takes away your sin. Please do not hold fast to it and do not hide from Me because - don't you see that My love overcomes everything? You are weighted down in this sinfulness. Allow Me this once, this night, to take your sin, to heal your heart. I give you my peace (Fr. extends hands out toward congregation.) You are overcome by your sin. Sin can never overcome me. I LOVE YOU.

Thursday, September 12, 1991

Our Lady's message:

My dear children, live in simpleness, simple ways and loving ways. Always seek to be calm, taking day by day. Oh, my children of God, blessed are you who follow in simpleness. Seek purity and live good, not bad ways. I bless you this evening with the grace from God. Strive to be simple. My message is to love and be simple. Do not try to understand, simply live day by day in my Son's light. Thank you for responding to my call.

Our Lord's message through Fr. Jack:

My dear ones, as I call you to follow Me, I see so often your trying to understand. My dear ones, what I say to you now, what I said to those when I was walking here with them here on earth does not always make sense to your human mind and understanding. I invite you this night, once again, to trust Me, your Lord and Savior. I do have words of everlasting life for you, and what I ask of you does not make sense to the world. What I ask of you makes sense only when you listen with your heart through My Spirit which is in you; I say to you this night - I give you My peace to calm your mind. I invite you to obedience and to trust. They will lead you into My heart. I LOVE YOU, I LOVE YOU, AND I AM WITH YOU ALWAYS.

Thursday, September 19, 1991

Our Lady's message:

My dear children, praise be my Son. My dear ones, please seek intimacy with my Son. He loves because He is love. He loves you and calls you to His mystical love. Oh, my dear ones, Satan is desperately trying to present you temptations and confusion. Know that as you focus on my Son that your temptations can only be short lived. Always seek God and live in His goodness like little children and you shall be protected. I bless you with the grace of God and I thank you for responding to my call.

Our Lord's message through Fr. Jack:

My dear ones, I love you. This night I look into your hearts and I see the desire that you have there to love and to serve My heavenly Father. I also see how often you become discouraged by your lack of love and your lack of response. Please, my dear ones, I invite you to give Me this night even the little love that you have in your heart, and I will make that little love grow. Do not be discouraged, your journey is not over yet. I am with you to encourage you, to protect you and to love you. Come with your doubt, come with your worry, come with your little love into my arms and rest, and love. You are mine! (Hands extended toward congregation and then to heart) I bless you, heal you of your lack of love. Please accept this healing from me this night.

Thursday, October 3, 1991

Our Lady's message:

My dear children, peace to you and praise to God. Oh My dear children, take time to absorb the love of My Son . Take time to allow Him to dwell in your being, bringing you His fruits of grace. Please My dear ones, Oh how loving He is and how He wishes you His tranquillity of peace. Allow yourselves to be loved by one another. Allow others to take care of you with their loving ways, and please allow My Son to love you and dwell peacefully. Thank you, my dear ones for responding to My call of peace and love within your lives.

Thursday, October 10, 1991

Our Lady's message:

— NO MESSAGE GIVEN TONIGHT —

Our Lord's message through Fr. Jack:

My dear ones, I give to you this night because you asked Me to be here. You invite Me with your heart. My Heavenly Father sent Me to you again. My dear ones, this night I make a request to you with your love to show other people how much I, your Jesus of Mercy, want to be with them also. Show them that My being with you here is not exclusive, but because you have invited Me. Please, my dear ones, help them to see by your joy and your love that My being with them is as simple as their inviting Me to be with them. It is the desire of My heart. I love you. I thank you for inviting Me in. I will always be with you. You are not alone. Please show others that they do not have to be alone either. I long to take all of My children into My embrace, and to My heart. You are the ones who can help Me. For this purpose, I bless you this night again with My joy, and My peace, and My mercy. Bring those again to all whom you meet.

Thursday, October 17, 1991

Our Lady's message:

My dear children, I ask you this night to rededicate yourselves to my Immaculate Heart and to my Son's Most Sacred Heart. You, my little ones, shall be put to the test. It is through your daily struggles that you grow. Pray with renewed vigor. Please pray, pray, pray. It brings me great joy to see you gathered to pray.

I bless you and thank you for your response to my call.

Our Lord's message through Fr. Jack:

My dear ones, I come to you this night to say plainly I am never separated from My Cross. My Father raised Me from the dead and yet, My dear ones, I still bear the wounds of My Crucifixion. Just as I, in that way, am never separated from My Cross, so are you never separated from yours. Dear ones, please listen - do not try to separate Me from My Cross. Do not try to separate yourself from your cross. Together we continue to save the world. My wounds, My dear ones, are now glorified. I, this night, glorify your wounds through mine. Your woundedness is not defeat but hope, encouragement and life for this world. I embrace you as you embrace your cross. I give you strength and courage to continue to bear it. I bless you this night again with the mercy that comes through My wounds from My Cross. I invite you, in turn, to shed that same mercy through your woundedness from your cross to others. I AM ALWAYS WITH YOU!

Thursday, October 24, 1991

Our Lady's message:

— NO MESSAGE GIVEN —

Our Lord's message through Fr. Jack:

My dear ones, I am here this night with you to bestow upon you, each of you, My healing mercy. Open your heart to receive this gift. This is the gift that will truly heal you for eternity. This is the gift that I bought for each of you on the cross. This is the gift that will bring you from where you are to Me. Allow this gift to wrap you in My love. As you receive My Mercy, as you allow it to heal you, you will begin to see what really matters. I tell you, My dear ones, you are still concerned with the wrong things. Allow My mercy to calm you, to relieve your anxiety, and to restore the joy that My Father has placed within you from the very moment of your conception. As a reminder of that joy, I continue to give you My Mother. I love you. I love you.

Thursday, October 31, 1991

Our Lady's message:

My dear children, praised be my Son. My dear little ones, never give up hope in my Son. Be strong in your faith. Put on your shield of armor. Never lose focus of your Jesus, your God. The evil one is desperately trying to ruin your happiness through despair. Satan is trying to interrupt my plan, but he cannot because God exists, and God is with me. Focus on my Son. The war is a war against God. Live in simpleness and never lose sight of the truth. Pray, pray, and live in simpleness. Bless you, my dear little children, and thank you for responding to my call.

Our Lord's message through Fr. Jack:

My dear ones, I am with you this night to encourage you on your way of holiness. I look at your heart and at everything else. I see that spark of My Holy Spirit and the Spirit of My Father. I encourage you, My dear ones, fan that spark into a flame to be My holy ones, My lights to this world. My affection and my love for you is limitless. I ask you to begin to realize how much I, your Lord, depend upon you in your holiness to touch those to whom I send you. My dear ones, it is I who touch them, it is I .... If you were to ask me for one thing this night, I encourage you to ask for holiness. This is the gift that I give. You are My holy ones - be joyful with this gift, and know that I AM ALWAYS WITH YOU!

Thursday, November 7, 1991

Our Lady's message:

My dear children, pray, pray, love. Please strive to restore love, mercy, compassion, respect, dignity and honesty, as my Son has asked.

Our Lord's message through Fr. Jack:

My dear ones, you belong to Me. I have come to you to find My lost ones. Many of you were lost, but you chose to begin to listen to My love and now you are found. I come this night to give you courage to realize you are Mine, and to ask you to find my lost ones. Find them by your mercy; find them by your love and compassion. They will be attracted to you as lead is to a magnet because they do not want to be lost, but they are so very lost. I give you again this night the love of My heart. My dear ones, you were lost and now you are home. This gift is there for all to receive. Through you, it is being offered again to all. I thank you, I love you. I am with you to bring the lost ones home!

Thursday, November 14, 1991

Our Lady's message:

Please unite in the graces of my Son. Know the evil one is attempting to destroy the love of mankind. Be children of God and do not lose your focus on God. He is your protection. He gives you life. Fight as soldiers of God for God. Begin now, my dear ones, to put your armor of love on. Be prepared for the battle is against God. Pray, Pray, Pray.

Our Lord's message through Fr. Jack:

My dear ones, I am here with you this night to speak again not to your mind but to your heart. So many reject My love, and My mercy, and My forgiveness. When they reject those gifts, then they reject My reign in their heart. They continue to search, but they will never find Me because they look in the wrong place and do the wrong thing. My dear ones, as I look into your hearts this night, I want to tell you again that My kingdom is already in you. When you accept My mercy, when you accept My love, when you accept My forgiveness, you experience My reign over you. Live now in My kingdom so that you can live fully when My kingdom is complete. I give you this night the strength to open your heart and to allow more and more of My kingdom to surround you. Know that you who are living in My kingdom will be the example to those I send you. I love you. You fill Me with joy this night and so I fill you with My joy this night.

Thursday, November 21, 1991

Our Lady's message:

My dear children, live by the way of humility, love, silence and discernment. Be prudent and always focus on my Son. He is not in a far away place. He is here, my dear children. Be the little children of God and hope in my Son. Please, please, pray for peace of mankind. Your humanity is now in danger. I bless you, my dear ones. Thank you for responding to my call.

Our Lord's message:

— NO MESSAGE GIVEN TONIGHT —

Thursday, December 5, 1991

Our Lady's message:

My dear children, I, your mother, come in sorrow; sorrow for mankind's lack of love. My dear ones, as my Son's mercy pours out into this world, my sorrow is for those lost souls who choose to walk away from Him; and it pierces my Immaculate Heart. Oh, how my Son still bears the wounds of humanity for your salvation. Please, my dear ones, pray and love. Your prayer finds a gracious hearing with my Son. Love. Your love dresses my Son's wounds who loves you and desires your love. Thank you, my dear ones, for responding to my call in these days of sorrow.

Our Lord's message through Fr. Jack:

I come this night to thank you for putting My words into practice, for responding to the invitation that My Mother has given to you. This night, my dear ones, My heart overflows with joy and with sadness. With joy because of you. Do you not realize that the very gift of prayer is a grace from My Heavenly Father to you? That very grace of prayer is offered to each one. That is why I say this night My heart is overflowing with joy and with sorrow. With joy because you accept this grace, this very grace of prayer for this world; in sorrow because so many still choose not to accept this grace, choose not to follow and put into practice My words, choose not only not to accept My Mother's invitation, but to mock her. Do they not know when they mock her, they mock Me? She is My heart. Thank you for loving her so much. When you love her, you love Me. My dear ones, this night I give you My peace and the gratitude of your Jesus. I thank you. I love you. I AM WITH YOU ALWAYS!

Thursday, December 12, 1991

Our Lady's message:

My dear children, I, your mother of joy, celebrate your years of prayer. Please, my dear little children, continue your prayers. The blessings of God is upon you. Look to Him for joy, peace, hope, truth mercy and humility. I thank you, my dear beloved ones, for your prayers which this world is in so much need. Bless you, and please continue. I shall be here because my Son is here and He loves you. Prepare for my festival in thanksgiving to God for allowing me to be here since December 19, 1989.

Thank you for responding to my call.

Our Lord's message through Fr. Jack:

My dear ones, I come to you this night to say to you how blessed are you among all people. How blessed are you for you have My Mother who is always with you, not only because she obeys the Father's command, but because she also wishes to be with you. She loves you so. My dear ones, thank you for loving her, thank you for loving her. When you love her, you love Me yourself. We have blessed you with her presence.

Thank you for accepting this blessing for it will not go away. It will last until I come. I give you My peace and My mercy.

Thursday, December 19, 1991

Our Lady's message:

My dear children, I give to you the rose of my heart which is the rose of my Son, His Heart. Oh, my dear little children, do not despair but rejoice in my Son, your Savior. Pray always for peace. Peace shall come if you are committed to love and compassion for a peaceful humanity. Your prayers can mitigate what is coming according to God, so form together in unity and pray, pray, pray! In thanksgiving, I thank God for His loving kindness, love and goodness He extends to you to allow me to be here with you. I shall continue to be here because of your generosity and love to one another. Thank you, my dear ones, for allowing this to be the center of my Son's divine mercy. I bless you and thank you for your response to my call.

Our Lord's message through Fr. Jack:

My dear ones, I ask you again tonight to trust in God. My Father sends Me to you to ask you to trust. Those things which so often cause you anxiety, those things which so often trouble your heart, those are the things in which you do not trust God. I remind you, My dear ones, that nothing is impossible to My Father, or to Me. I encourage you to live your life to give honor to My Father; and, when you are tempted to fear, know that I am with you. I encourage you to take My hand. I will never let go of you. You are in My Heart. I love you. Trust, believe, have courage. I give you this night My peace. Allow this gift, My dear ones, to surround your very souls.

January 9, 1992

Our Lady's message:

My dear children, I come to you because of the goodness of My Son who has allowed me to be here with you. He is here with you, my dear ones, and His divine mercy flows out unto you. My dear ones, please unite. Please be peaceful with one another and loving. Pray, pray, pray, my little children. Reflect His love in your actions and words. My dear ones, this is the age of my Son's mercy. Please allow His love and mercy to dwell in you through openness. Focus on Him and He will guide you in love. Thank you, my dear ones, for responding to my call.

Thursday, January 16, 1992

Our Lady's message:

My dear children, peace to you always. My dear little ones, please pray and let the goodness of God never leave you, that you will always remain obedient and loving little children. Please, my children, focus on my Son. Trust in Him. Trust, trust, trust. Do not judge one another harshly. Always seek to please God by loving one another. Be cautious that you may hurt someone because of lack of humility. Love through trusting and obedience to God. I bless you, my dear ones. Please be cautious of your hidden pride. Place my Son first always. He is the only one to give you comfort, joy and peace. Thank you for responding to my call.

Our Lord's message through Fr. Jack:

My dear ones, I come to you this night to tell you again I love you, and to invite you again to acceptance - the acceptance of My Father's will for you. My dear ones, only in that acceptance of His will comes the peace for which you seek and the joy that your soul is so much in need of. They go hand-in-hand. Many times you believe that if you accept My Father's will, that will bring pain and suffering to you. I present to you this night My Cross. Do not be afraid of MY Cross. Embrace the cross and you will embrace My Father's will for you. Through that cross comes joy, and peace, and salvation. I give you My mercy to wipe out the fear in your heart. I am with you. I AM ALWAYS WITH YOU!

Thursday, January 23, 1992

Our Lady's message:

My dear children, I come to ask you to pray and to love. I come because my Son is love, and He loves you all, His beloved children. My dear little ones, begin first to love your family. Be love to one another, then you can love your fellow brethren. Please beware that Satan is trying to cause division and disrupt unity not only in the family, but in the world. Form together in love as a strong unit and you will have the shield to protect you against his attempts. I love you, my little ones, and bless you in the name of my Son. Thank you for responding to my call.

Our Lord's message:

— NO MESSAGE GIVEN TONIGHT —

Thursday, January 30, 1992

Our Lady's message:

My dear little ones, I, your mother of joy, come to comfort you and bless you in the name of my Son. My dear children, be calm little children, loving and at peace. The control you wish to have can only be the control my Son gives you in His peace and love. Surrender to Him and trust Him. He will guide you and crown you with His love. Dear, dear children, pray for surrendering and to be the open vessels of my Son's love. I bless you, my dear ones. Thank you for your response to my call.

Our Lord's message through Fr. Jack:

My dear ones, I ask you this night for your faithfulness and your perseverance. Please allow Me, your Jesus, to be your God. Trust Me please. I ask for your faithfulness and your perseverance because with those I will be able to touch you. Without faithfulness you block My touch. I am here with you. I am with you wherever you are. Please allow Me to be your God. As you allow this through your faithfulness and perseverance, then you will be able to receive the gifts that I offer to you and I long to give you - peace, compassion and My mercy! I thank you for your devotion. I know, my dear ones, it is not easy. That is why I am with you and that is why My Mother is here. You are never alone. You are mine and I love you!

Thursday, February 6, 1992

Our Lady's message:

My dear children, do not be preoccupied with worry. Trust in my Son. Surrender unto Him all your worries, concerns and fears and be at peace. You are weak in your humanness, but strong in my Son. Seek to serve Him faithfully, being obedient and loving in following His ways. He has taught you. I love you, my dear little children. I am your Mother of Joy to bring you the joy of my Son. I bless you and thank you for responding to my call.

Our Lord's message:

My dear ones, I come to you this night to speak to you once again of the simplicity of following My call. My dear ones, I invite you to trust, trust in Me and in My Father and in Our Holy Spirit. When you trust, then fear disappears. I want for you the peace that I am so willing to give you. You will experience this peace in simplicity. My words to you have never been complicated. They have been plain and simple; and when you listen to them with your heart, you know the truth. I love you and I encourage you this night to simplicity in following My call. I AM ALWAYS, ALWAYS WITH YOU!

Thursday, February 13, 1992

Our Lady's message:

My dear children, please pray for my priests. Pray, pray, pray. Never cease praying. Do not cause division but unite in harmony and be obedient to my beloved Pope. Please, my little children, pray that division does not result from lack of love, and power of human ways. This will only deepen the sorrow of my heart. I love you, my dear ones, and I bless you in the name of my Son. Thank you for responding to my call.

Our Lord's message:

—NO MESSAGE GIVEN TONIGHT.—

Thursday, February 20, 1992

Our Lady's message:

My dear children, I am here because my Son is here. I am not leaving because my Son is here and He is not leaving. His divine mercy and love is flowing out unto you and all your beloved ones. Oh, my dear little ones, NO obstacle is too great for my Son. Give to Him your fears, anxieties and worries. Open and surrender to Him. Please, my dear ones, as you receive my Son this night, be intimate with Him so that He can fill you with discernment and His peace. I bless you, my dear little children. Thank you for responding to my call.

Our Lord's message through Fr. Jack:

My dear ones, I come to you again this night to speak to your heart. I remind you that I, your Lord and Savior, do not look at your outward trappings, I look at your heart. Please believe Me when I say to you - I love you as you are. So often I see that you do not love yourself. My dear ones, I accept you as you are at this moment. I love you, YOU, not your actions. I see that you look so often at your actions and you are over-come by your weaknesses and by your sinfulness. My dear ones, only when you love and accept yourself as you are and offer yourself to me AS YOU ARE, only then will My love for you be able to flow into your very heart. Again, I say to you, believe that I love you, believe that I love you so much that even now I will do anything not to have you separated from Me. Accept My love and offer Me this night yourself. I take you all in My embrace. YOU ARE MINE!

Thursday, February 27, 1992

Our Lady's message:

My dear children, I come to be here with you because I come with my Son. I bless you this night. Please, my dear ones, FOCUS completely on my Son. If you are totally immersed in His love, focusing on Him, all your disturbances would dissi-pate because you would be in His peace. You cannot control, my dear ones, because my Son is here. Even if you think you are right, and are not correct, the truth of my Son's light would be made known. Therefore, focus totally on Him and do not allow trivial disturbances to disrupt your peace. Focus and pray, pray, pray. Thank you for responding to my call.

Our Lord's message through Fr. Jack:

My dear ones, I come tonight to you to invite you to give Me, your Lord, the totality of your heart. Allow Me to be your wealth. I see how hard you try and how so often distraction clouds your vision of Me. My dear ones, I am with you now and forever. I am as close to you as your heart because you have invited Me to be your heart. I love you and because of my love for you, I give you My Kingdom. Pray, persevere! I am with you. I give you this night the love, and the healing, and the strength. I gift you Myself and I take your heart and present it to My Father. Be at peace. I calm your worried heart.

Thursday, March 5, 1992

Our Lady's message:

My dear children, I came to ask you for reconciliation. I, your Mother, see so many broken hearts. Please be open to begin more time for confessions here at this parish for all my children coming. My priests, I call from afar, please be open to assisting My chosen pastor in making this available for My children to receive this most beautiful sacrament. It is necessary here at my Son's Center of His Divine Mercy so that He can free you and heal you. Please by obedient to this, my Son's request. I love you, my dear little children, and bless you in the name of He who sent me. Pray and prepare for your new beginning through confession. Thank you for responding to this my Son's call.

Our Lord's message through Fr. Jack:

My dear little ones, I come to you this night to ask you choose life. My dear ones, I do not wish that you die. I came and I am now here to offer you life in the fullest measure. Choose life by choosing to follow Me, your Jesus. You follow Me, my dear ones, by giving up your sinfulness. You see, your sinfulness blocks you from My loving embrace because you have chosen to embrace a thing or a person instead of Me. My dear ones, embrace Me. Live! I gift you this night the grace and the strength you need to turn from sin. Come, embrace Me, so that I may embrace you and you will live forever with Me. Don't give up. Take My hand. I am with you. During these days I give you My Mother in a very special way. Use her as your example of choosing life. I love her! I love her! SHE BRINGS YOU TO ME! I LOVE HER!

Thursday, March 12, 1992

Our Lady's message:

My dear children, seek a private and personal intimacy with my Son. He desires your love and for an intimate quiet relationship with each one of you. My dear little children, do not delay in running to my Son. Use the most blessed Sacrament of Confession and trust that your journey is in the best hands. My dear children, during this season, do not be somber or afraid but rejoice that my Son is your Savior and believe it. Trust in Him. Use the Sacrament please, my dear ones, of Reconciliation; and trust, pray, pray, love and surrender in peace unto my Son. Thank you, my children, for responding to my call.

Our Lord's message through Fr. Jack:

My dear ones, I am here with you, your Jesus of Mercy. You are not alone, never alone. I am with you! Our Holy Spirit is within you always! I send My angels to guard you and, in this time, I have even sent My Mother to be with you. My Father gives you these gifts because He loves you. He invites you again, over and over again to believe in His love. I give you this night the grace of My mercy and I touch your heart. I invite you to come into My heart and to be at peace with Me. Now you can go because you are strengthened. You have nothing to fear. I AM WITH YOU!!

Thursday, March 19, 1992

Our Lady's message:

My dear children, as I read your hearts this night, I bless you and invite you to allow me to comfort your sadness. My dear little ones, your trials and tribulations shall pass. Receive them in joy, not in sadness. See my Son as your strength. Please, little ones, it is time to pray, not to cry. Trust, again I say, trust in my Son. Do not be afraid. I am here and my Son is here, so be at peace as my Son molds you into His beautiful creation. Blessings on you and thank you for responding to my call.

Our Lord's message through Fr. Jack:

My dear ones, I am here with you this night to invite you to be My disciples of hope. I see in the hearts of My people a lack of that gift that I wish to give them, as I give it to you. And so, I invite you to live in the spirit of hope for the world, to be signs for them of My salvation, to be signs for them, that through their suffering, there is joy. My dear ones, you will only be disciples of hope as you become obedient to My Father, as I was obedient not only to My Father but to my dear, dear Joseph. Without obedience there is no hope. I love you and thank you for listening to Me. Your effect on those to whom I send you is already having a wonderful end. I bless you this night, my dear ones, and I strengthen your hope as I strengthen your obedience. Together we are obedient always to God, Our Father.

Thursday, March 26, 1992

Our Lady's message:

My dear children, reach out to one another. Be kind, and loving, and compassionate. You are sharp with one another judging, and you need to love. Focus on my Son, and you will be molded in His love so that you will be able to love each other. Do not focus on your skepticism or worry about who is right or who is wrong. But if you focus on your own journey with my Jesus, you will have peace and He will guide you. God's Will will be done and His truth will be revealed. Please love, my little ones. I bless you and take your petitions to my Son. Thank you for responding to my call.

Our Lord's message through Fr. Jack:

My dear ones, My Father again sends Me this night to you, as He has sent Me before to invite and to teach you, to draw you closer, to draw your world back to Him. I thank you this night for listening to My voice. You do not see Me, but you can hear Me. Thank you for listening. Thank you for accepting My presence here with you. Because of your acceptance, you are able to hear when I speak. I invite you this night to give to Me your pride-filled hearts which are full of hurt. Give them to Me, and I will heal them and give you new hearts. Because of your acceptance of My presence with you, My Father continues to allow Me to speak. He allows My Mother to be with you. Because of this blessing that you have given to My

Father, He blesses you this night through Me. He gives you the strength, and His grace, and His mercy. Because of your acceptance, these tremendous gifts go out from you to all. I love you. Thank you for allowing Me to touch your heart.

Thursday, April 2, 1992

Our Lady's message:

My dear children, I am your mother, your medium to my Son, Jesus, the Alpha and the Omega. My dear little ones, please pay attention to your own journey instead of helping others with their spiritual journey. My Jesus wishes to guide each of you personally on your own journey if you will allow Him. I protect you and prepare you in perfection for my Son. He will not deny you His love because He will not deny me, and I present you to Him like a little child. Please do not judge others of pridefulness when this is only harboring bitterness in your own hearts. They are truly humble, but it is your own pride surfacing. Therefore, please pay attention to your own walk with my Son, and He will purify you and grace you with His virtues. Thank you, my little ones, for responding to my call.

Our Lord's message through Fr. Jack:

My dear ones, I, your Jesus, am here with you this night because of the love of My Father whom I have told you is your Father also. He sends Me to you to plead on His behalf to invite you again to come to Him. You listen. My Father thanks you for listening. My dear ones, I ask that you pray for those who do not listen, who have filled themselves so full of themselves that they have no room for My Father's words. Listen as I speak to you within your heart. My dear ones, there is nothing to fear. Live what you have heard from Me who speaks only what My Father wishes. I am here this night to remind you not only of My love but of God the Father's love for you. I bless you with My mercy which is His mercy, with My peace which is His peace. WE LOVE YOU! WE LOVE YOU! WE LOVE YOU!

Thursday, April 9, 1992

Our Lady's message:

My dear children, I am your Mother of Joy because my Son is my Joy. He is your joy. Give to Him your hearts, dear ones. Please allow Him to comfort you, hold you and guide you in the only true journey to true happiness and eternal bliss. My dear little ones, God does exist. Unite now together in love. Do not wait for signs and wonders. If you wait, it will be too late. Turn now to my Son. During this week, go to my Son and immerse yourself into His Most Sacred Heart. The urgency is prayer and conversion to the truth NOW! Do not fear. There is no need to fear, but need to change. Thank you, my dear children, for responding to my call.

Our Lord's message through Fr. Jack:

My dear ones, I invite you to walk with Me this week the steps I took to gain your freedom. Embrace with Me the Cross, the sign of your freedom, and the covenant with God, My Father and yours, made again with you. As you embrace the Cross, you will also embrace the Resurrection. I love you! This week you will see again the depth of My love. You will experience again, when you open your hearts, the depth of My mercy. You need not fear the Cross. I am with you always - always with you. My dear little ones, come to Me and together we will go to My Father and to your Father. I love you. KNOW THAT I LOVE YOU! ç† é† . Do not wait for signs and wonders. If you wait, it will be too late. Turn now to my Son. During this week, go to my Son and immerse yourself into His Most Sacred Heart. The urgency is prayer and conversion to the truth NOW! Do not fear. There is no need to fear, but need to change. Thank you, my dear children, for responding to my call.

Our Lord's message through Fr. Jack:

My dear ones, I invite you to walk with Me this week the steps I took to gain

Thursday, April 23, 1992

Our Lady's message:

My dear little children, I come to give you the blessing of my Son. Please, focus on Him. Unite together and pray for peace. Please be loving. Satan is trying to cause division. Please be alert, my children. Pray, pray, pray. Join Me. Join together in love. Stop your bickering and judging of others. Pray, be silent and loving. Join with me. Reconcile, my children. I have asked three times now, from my Son, for the Sacrament of Reconciliation to take place here at His Center of Mercy. Please take action, reconcile and join to a peaceful end. I love you and bless you, my little children. Thank you for your response to my call.

Our Lord's message through Fr. Jack:

My dear ones, I am with you here and now! I, your Resurrected Lord, your Jesus of Mercy, am here. You say that you cannot see Me. I say to you do not look for Me with your eyes but with your heart. Go into the silence of your heart where I am waiting for you. There you will see Me. There will I embrace you and, in the silence, we are one. I invite you to come away with Me into your heart so that I may heal you, embrace you with My peace, and joy, and mercy. I AM HERE! I have always been with you since My Father raised Me from death to life. Allow Me to enliven you. Look and see with your heart. This night I touch your heart. I hold it so that you may come to Me, so that you may receive the embrace that I long to give to you. Be silent and see Me!

Thursday, April 30, 1992

Our Lady's message:

My dear children, pray for your enemies and bless those who persecute you. Allow the spirit of God to move through you out unto others. Any blessing you extend out to others will be returned to you if not received well from the other person. So send a loving prayer to your enemies, and that love and peace will only come to rest on you if not received in openness from those you pray for. Have mercy, my dear ones, have mercy. Mercy is the unquestionable proof of your love for God. Unite in love. I bless you in the name of my Son. Thank you for responding to my call.

Our Lord's message through Fr. Jack:

I come again this night to you, sent again by My Heavenly Father. I am with you. I say again this night to your heart — do not be afraid. Take My hand. I will never abandon you. I am with you now and will be with you always. Do not fear. Be with Me totally. I love you and I bless you with My presence which is My Spirit within you. You are strong because of the Holy Spirit. Peace! My mercy upon you this night.

Thursday, May 7, 1992

Our Lady's message:

My dear little children. those who are begotten of God conquer the world. You conquer through faith, love and trust in Him. My children, I come because my Son's love is upon you. Please unite and live in harmony. Be loving and kind. Be compassionate. Focus on Him. Thank the Father for it is His love that you are so beautiful. Pray, pray for peace and forgive one another. I bless you tonight in the name of my Son. Thank you for responding to my Son. Come now into His Most Sacred Heart. He awaits your love. Peace!

Our Lord's message through Fr. Jack:

My dear ones, I come to you this night to tell you that I am your life. I, your Jesus, am your food. I come to tell you of My love with all of My heart. I love you, each of you. I ask you — accept Me as your life, as your food. You are precious to Me. I bless you this night, the blessing that goes into your very soul — blessing and healing and mercy, compassion and joy, and truth and courage, and above all, hope and faith. I am with you. There is nothing at all to fear. Take My hand, I want to hold you.

Thursday, May 14, 1992

Our Lady's message:

— *NO MESSAGE WAS GIVEN TONIGHT* —

Our Lord's message given through Fr. Jack:

My dear ones, I am here with you again this night to remind you of My love, to invite you to accept that love again fully into your hearts. The love with which I love you is a selfless, self-sacrificing love. My Father gives Me again this night to you. I come to invite you to be My apostle of love. Each of you — each of you to love those to whom I send you to be My apostle of hope to those dear ones. Yes, my dear little ones, it will not be easy to love and to be hopeful unless you allow My love and My hope to be yours. I need you to touch your world. You are now My apostles, the ones I send. If you accept — if you accept, know that I am with you. I am always with you. Please believe Me when I say again, "I have chosen you." Pray to accept this invitation.

Thursday, May 21, 1992

Our Lady's message:

My dear little children, it brings me joy to see you praying. Pray! Pray! Pray! I take your prayers to Jesus Who presents you to the Father. My dear ones, prayer is the powerful tool to prevent dissension and confusion from the evil one. My children, please unite. Do not look at the past, but unite now in the moment and on going from this point together. Do not try to control or be stubborn. These only bring self destruction, not spiritual freedom. I love you, and bless you in the name of my Son. Thank you for responding to my call.

Our Lord's message through Fr. Jack:

My dear ones, I come to you this night to remind you that I have given you My joy. I wish you to have this gift of joy to the fullest measure. The reason you do not experience this joy is because so often you do not keep My Commandments. When you do not keep My Commandments, you block the joy that I give you. Instead of joy, you experience pain and confusion and chaos in your life. I, your Jesus of Mercy, beg you this night to keep My Commandments so that you may experience My joy. My Father and I send My mother to you under the title of Joy to remind you that this is the gift that you can have. My dear ones, I love you. When I see you not keeping My Commandments, when I see the pain and the confusion and the chaos that this causes in your life, it saddens Me. I tell you it doesn't have to be that way. This night I have reminded you of the way to possess this joy. Please listen and act on it. I strengthen you with My mercy to overcome your sinfulness, and I give you the gift of My peace.

Thursday, May 28, 1992

Our Lady's message:

My dear little children, in Jesus I love you and come in the blessings of my Son. Please, pray fervently and be at peace living in the moment. Be loving and patient. Tonight I pass on the special blessing of my Son to you. Embrace my Son by embracing one another in love. Unite and live in harmony. Pray, my little ones, pray! The evil one is trying to cause destruction. Only prayer and love are the swords to freedom and justice in God. I bless you in the name of my Son. Treasure Him. Love Him by loving one another. Thank you for responding to my call.

Our Lord's message through Fr. Jack:

— NO MESSAGE WAS GIVEN TONIGHT —

Thursday, June 4, 1992

Our Lady's message:

My dear children, Jesus loves you. He is my dear Son, my dear Jesus. In the midst of your world there are struggles and hardships, but all can be overcome because Jesus has overcome the world. My son exists amongst you and He is calling you to remove yourself from focusing on your hardship and the business of your life, but to focus on Him and trust in Him. All love is of Him and all must be yielded to Him in love to live in union with Him in His peace. I bless you, my little ones, and encourage you this night to give all of yourself to Jesus in commitment of love. There is nothing you risk when you give to Him your total being as He has given to you. Pray and love. Give to Him in love of yourself. He is real. Thank you for your response. Peace can exist if you begin to live peacefully and unselfishly. Blessings in the name of He who has sent me.

Our Lord's message through Fr. Jack:

My dear ones, I come to you this night to encourage you to speak the truth and to live the truth. This truth is the gift that I give to you with My Father and through Our Holy Spirit. You will know the truth as you listen with your heart to the ways in which My Father and Myself and Our Holy Spirit speak to you. You live My truth when you keep My Commandments. My dear ones, live simply, speak less and let your words always give honor and glory to My Father. I look upon you this night with the most tender love of My heart, and I see that you are yearning to be truly children of My Father. I tell you, one of the signs that you are truly children of God is that you live and speak the truth. In this world of the evil one's deceptions, you will stand out as a light as you live and speak the truth. I give you My strength to live this gift of truth. I touch your minds, and your lips, and your hearts, so that you may speak the truth of Our God, of My Father and your Father, and as you speak and live the truth, know that My Father and Our Holy Spirit and I are with you and within you, as close to you as your very breath.

Thursday, June 11, 1992

Our Lady's message:

My dear children, peace to you and blessings in the name of my Son. My dear ones, I need to continue to invite you to daily prayer and focus on my Son. Trust in Him. All will be well and you will live in His Most Sacred Heart if you love Him and allow Him to love you. Trust, my dear ones, and pray. Never cease praying. There is much destruction in the world, but Jesus is peace and love, if all unite and put aside trivial arguments. I love you and bless you in the name of Jesus. Peace. Thank you for responding to my call.

Our Lord's message through Fr. Jack:

My dear ones, I am here again with you this night to remind you that I am always in your heart. I invite you ever more to come to Me within your own heart to allow My presence to become more and more real to you. My dear ones, I am the gift that My Father gives to you. I invite you again to accept Me, your Savior and the Lord of your heart. Experience My presence within you as you pray, and together we will praise My Father and your Father. Pray, my dear ones, with your heart and you will find that I am with you. I bless you with My presence, with My peace and with My mercy.

Thursday, June 18, 1992

Our Lady's message through Fr. Jack:

My dear ones, I love you. My Jesus taught you how to pray. He has allowed me to come to you to invite you to pray with your heart. So often you say that you do not know how to pray. Listen to my Jesus speak to your hearts. Listen as my spouse, the Holy Spirit speaks to your heart. They will again teach you. Come and pray. I invite you even more this night to pray. Please believe me when I say to you how valuable prayer from your heart is. Your prayer is capable of changing not only events but the hardest of hearts as well. I am with you here, and wherever you go I will pray with you. I invite you to pray with me. I love you, my dear little ones, with the love of a mother's heart. I embrace you and draw each of you close to my heart, my heart which is my Son, Jesus. May His name be praised now and forever more.

Our Lord's message:

— NO MESSAGE WAS GIVEN TONIGHT —

Thursday, July 2, 1992

Our Lord's message through Fr. Jack:

My dear ones, as you come here this night to pray, so many ask for healing. I tell you, my dear ones, I wish to heal all of you, but what each of you needs healing of most, you very seldom ask for healing. That area is the area of your sin. Your sin destroys you; your sin paralyzes you; your sin is the cancer of your soul. My dear ones, I ask you and invite you now to give to Me your sin so that I may heal you truly. I love you. I have died for you; My Father has raised Me up for you. It is truly simple, my dear ones, stop sinning and you will be healed - healed in your spirit, healed within your heart. Do not be discouraged, by your sin. Offer your sin to Me. I will heal you. I love you and bless you this night with My peace, with My forgiveness, and with My mercy.

Thursday, July 23, 1992

Our Lord's message through Fr. Jack:

My dear ones, I come this night to remind you again that I am here. I am with you. At times, because you have chosen to be your own god, you do not experience Me. My little ones, open your hearts. Open your hearts so that you may understand that I, your Jesus, wish to be the Lord in your heart so that I may lead you back to God. My dear ones, when you are so preoccupied with yourselves, with your selfishness, with your pride, and with your pain, I cannot be the Lord in your heart. I love you and I extend again My arms to you. I am here with you. I am with you in your heart. Allow Me to be your Lord once more. Give me this night the pride, the selfishness, the pain, so that I may once again reign in your heart; and then we, together, will go to My Father. Peace and joy, my dear ones.

* * * * * * * * * * * * * *

At the end of the prayer service Fr. Jack announced that Our Lady wanted us to know that:

'She is so very grateful this night for your prayers. She loves you. She is so pleased and happy to see you praying.'

Thursday, July 30. 1992

Our Lord's message:

My Dear Ones:

I come this night to tell you that you are not useless to My Father nor to Me. You are precious to Me, each of you, and to My Father, to your Father. You are beautiful to Us. We love you. I ask you this night to allow Our Holy Spirit to mold your heart. To mold it, to form it, and to offer it to God Our Father. To each of you who are here I bless with My grace and the grace of God Our Father. Know that in the remolding of your heart, although it will be painful at times, I am there. I love you and bless you and take you, each of you, to My Heart.

Thursday, August 6, 1992

Our Lady's message through Mary Cook:

My Dear Children, PRAY! PRAY! PRAY! Oh my dear ones, I need your prayers in this critical time of my plan. Please, continue to open your hearts to my Son. Continue to surrender your own wills to the Divine Will of the Father. My little, little children, I love you so! You fill me with so much joy as you pray for all the lost souls of your world! I love you! Peace to you! Thank you for responding to my call.

Thursday, August 13, 1992

Our Lady's message through Mary Cook:

My dear little, little children, be not afraid! Know that my Son and I are guiding you. Please continue to take hold of our hands and allow us to lead you down the path of salvation. What is needed now is trust and much prayer! I love you, my little ones, and know I am your mother! Thank you for responding to my call.

August 27.1992

Our Lady's message to the world through Gianna Talone: St. Maria Goretti Parish, Scottsdale, Arizona

My dear children, I urge your close attention as My Son has allowed me to be here. Please my little ones, put aside your falsehoods and fears. There is too much negativity acting as a catalyst to human destruction. I invite you instead to draw closer to one another in prayer. Renew prayer in your family and devotion to spending more time with Jesus. It is urgent. There are great struggles about to unfold. Division in families is leading to division in the church. Reconciliation is urgent. I have asked prayer, conversion, penance and initially you took the steps to procure your relationship with God but are reverting to old ways. I have asked obedience to My Pope but division is resulting. The need for prayer, reconciliation. harmony, love and conversion is URGENT NOW! Renounce what is preventing you in your spiritual growth. Read the Holy Scripture and listen to the Holy Spirit speak the message of My

Son. Begin right now to solidify your relationship with God by loving yourselves and restoring your self respect. Cease from running from yourselves. You cannot love your countrymen if you do not love yourself. You are walking ways of power instead of love. The greatest sin is that which destroys love. This is urgent. The effects of this wickedness is causing jealousy, hatred, killings and divisions. War, power struggles and economical warfare's are surfacing from lack of love. My Son is tired, very tired. The faith to God is forgotten. The time is coming when every man and woman on this earth will know that God exists. All will have a glimpse at the state of their soul. Those seconds will seem like eternity. Your love of gold and silver is about to become glittering dust and be swept away. Spiritual warfare exists in the heavens and you must now live in the perfection of your faith. The wicked are convinced they are invisible, but they are not. Do not be afraid. To all His faithful ones God PROMISES victory over the powers of evil and the world. Know my Iittle ones that only God can make you holy. You can receive Gods seal on your soul only by abandoning your will to Him. God's love will shower you and replace everything if you accept it. Bless you my little ones and thank you for responding to my URGENT call.

Our Lord's message though Fr. Jack:
St. Maria Goretti Parish, Scottsdale, Arizona

August 27, 1992

My dear beloved ones, I come this night from My Father to encourage you and to invite you again to continue your journey. There is nothing that you need to fear. I am with you, always. I am with you when you are alone. I am with you when you are with your families. I am with you at work. I am with you at school. I am with you all the time, everywhere. My dear ones, what is there for you to fear? Nothing, there is nothing for you to fear. Do you fear death? By dying I have conquered death for you. Are you in fear because of your sins? My dear ones, by dying I destroyed sin and the hold that sin would have upon you. I have conquered everything. And yet I know my dear ones, how difficult it is for you because you do not see Me. I am here to tell you that you are looking for Me in the wrong place. Come to Me in my Blessed Sacrament; I am there. Listen to Me through the Sacred Scripture; I am there. And if you allow yourselves the quiet that I would give you, you will find Me within your heart. There is nothing to fear. This night I bless you and ask you to give to Me again your heart for I give you Mine. Peace, mercy, My strength, the joy of our Holy Spirit is with you always.

Thursday, September 3, 1992

Our Lady's message:

My dear children. I am your mother who comes tonight to wrap you in my mantle of love. Oh, my children, PLEASE do not fear. Fear is useless, my little ones. Pray for peace, peace in your own hearts. By praying for peace, you can conquer any fear or temptation. I love you, my little ones! Please pray for peace for yourselves, and you will bring that peace to the whole world.

Our Lord's message through Fr. Jack:

My dear ones. I come to you this night — I, your merciful Lord, to ask and to invite you again to put Me first in your life so that I may lead you to My Father who is your Father. My dear little ones, I see in your heart so much worry for others, so much sadness for others. I tell you if only you will pray and allow Me to be the center, and no one else, the center of your heart, I would then be able to take care of those for whom you worry and those who are causing you sadness. My dear ones, please take care of yourself and your relationship with Me. Allow that to be the most important thing in your life, and you will then be truly children of My Father. This night I offer you, if you would only take My strength, to give up the worry for others. My dear, dear ones, don't you understand that if you are worried you will be distracted? I love those for whom you worry and those who cause you sadness more than you could possibly imagine. Give them to Me. This night especially give Me again your heart. I give you My mercy, I give you My peace, and I give you again this night My heart — My mother! I love you! I love you! My dear ones, truly MY LOVE IS ALL YOU NEED!

Thursday, September 10, 1992

Our Lady's message:

My dear children, I am your Mother of Joy, but also your Mother of Sorrows. I see your pain and your sufferings, my little ones. I ask you to unite your tears with the most precious blood of my Son's Passion. I ask you to allow Him to soften your hearts and to allow your purification to continue. I love you, my dear children. Please continue to pray for the lost souls of the world. Peace to you.

Our Lord's message through Fr. Jack:

My dear ones. I come to you this night to say one thing to you — I wish to encourage you in your following Me. My Commandment of love is not easy for you. As you draw closer to Me, I will be able to love more through you; but it is not easy, my dear ones. It truly is a labor — a labor of love. There are people in your life who are easy to love — cherish them, but there are also people in your life who are not easy to love. Those are the ones, my dear ones, to whom I send you. I will love them through you. I will be with you. I will strengthen you. You will not be alone. I was rejected when I tried to love. My dear ones, so too will you be rejected. Cling to Me and even the rejection will not be as painful. Know that to love is My commandment still for you. This night I touch that part of your heart which has been hurt as you attempted to love and have been rejected. I heal you and bless you and take you to My heart. My dear ones, I, your Lord, love you and I will never reject you.

Thursday, September 17, 1992

Our Lady's message:

My dear children. I continue to call you to unity and harmony. The evil one is trying desperately to cause division, and work in every circumstance towards deception and darkness. If you would listen and act on what I ask, you will be protected from all harm. Begin practicing and living my words to you in your own life. Do not be fearful and do not dwell on negativity. Instead, abandon fully to my Son. Nothing is safer than the way of self abandonment. True faith allows you to accept with joy everything that happens. If you abandon unto my Son, the results will be glorious. God will grace you in every moment to act virtuously. God's action is boundless in scope and power. Empty yourselves so my Son can fill you. Thank you, my little ones; my blessings in the name of my Son and His peace. To His name be praise and glory. Thank you for responding to my call.

Our Lord's message through Fr. Jack:

My dear ones, I come this night as your Lord and Savior, the Jesus of Mercy whom you follow, to ask again, to invite once again that you love Me. My dear ones, the way you love Me is to pray. This simple request — in fulfilling it you show your love for Me. I see so many of you, you are so busy about so many things, even busy about holy things, but in your busyness you are putting prayer aside. My dear ones. pray first, and always, and during, and last. I know you do not understand the power of prayer, of your prayer. My mother has told you, and is telling you, and begged you to pray. I, your Lord, ask you now — pray, rededicate your lives to prayer. It is truly, my dear ones, believe Me, the most important thing that you can do for anyone, that you can do for the world. It is the holiest of holy works. I ask you this night to put prayer back into the place where it belongs in your life. I know too, my dear ones, how taxing it may be, but if you do it for Me you will experience My peace and My joy, and you will then be able to see clearly what truly I am asking of you in your lives. I bless you with My love, I bless you and your family with My mercy.

Thursday, September 24, 1992

Our Lady's message:

My dear little children, a holy soul is one which freely submits to God's will. By the help of His grace self abandonment will follow. Live in peace and do not be frightened. Know for certain that God is guiding you. You may not understand or see clearly God's works; but, if you abandon unto Him, you will see clearly the action of His grace. God loves you, my little ones. He is love and love inspires you to perform your duties faithfully and with love. Pray for His strength of joy and offer your distress with joy to God. You may not understand His methods or solve His puzzles, but you will attain full beauty and rejoice as He conquers your despair. Bless you, my little ones. and thank you for responding to my call.

Our Lord's message:

— NO MESSAGE RECEIVED FROM OUR LORD TONIGHT —

Thursday, October 1, 1992

Our Lady's message through Gianna Talone:

My dear children, do not be upset or worried from the humiliation which comes from this present world. Shelter in our God and enjoy Him who lives in you. You can benefit from your weaknesses and failures, fears and doubts, by drawing good from your infirmities. My Son wishes to be your only nourishment and desire. God is your only sole support and only means of achieving holiness. Thank you, my dear little ones, for responding to my call. Peace to you. Blessings from my Son is upon you.

Our Lord's message through Fr. Jack:

My dear ones, I invite you this night to come to Me as children of My Father. I ask you again this night to trust in His will for you as I trusted, as My mother trusted. This trust will assist you in living as the children of God. I am here with you to remind you of the love My Father has for you. He sent Me once and now He sends Me again. I am with you. I tell you I love you also. Dear children of My Father? I bless you with My peace and with My mercy.

October 8, 1992

Our Lady's message through Gianna Talone:

My dear little children, I your Mother of Joy have come for a purpose. My little ones I am the Mother of this country. This is my country and I need your help. As you seek me, I also seek your help. Please, my little ones, there needs to be great conversion and change of hearts. Unity and harmony. I need you. You are the ones that can change this country's situation and be the catalyst for change in the world. Pray, Pray, Pray. Take heed to change your hearts and return back to God. Be living examples of God's word. Live the Gospel. Live my Son's words. I bless you, my little ones, and ask for your help. Thank you for responding to my call.

Our Lord's message through Fr. Jack:

My dear ones, I am here with you. I, your Jesus of Mercy, to tell you again this night of My love for you and to remind you that you are not alone. I bless you this night with My mercy. My dear ones, I see your hearts. I see your hearts not as you see them but as My Father sees them, and I take your hearts to My heart to heal them, to strengthen them, to give them again joy and hope. I ask you to persevere in your love, to persevere in the hope that I give you, to persevere in your prayer. I am with you. You are children of My Father. We love you. We love you.

October 15, 1992

Our Lady's message through Mary Cook:

My Dear Children, I am your Mother! Please PRAY, PRAY, PRAY! Pray for Jesus to put the DESIRE to sacrifice in your heart! To sacrifice for your sins and the lost souls of your world! Please my children, be humble and obedient! Please pray and sacrifice for the love of my Jesus! I love you. Peace to you! Thank you for listening to my words.

Our Lord's message:

—NO MESSAGE WAS GIVEN THROUGH FATHER JACK THIS EVENING.—

October 22, 1992

Message from Our Lady Given to Gianna:

My dear children, do not set limits on the will of God. The will of God is the life of the body and the soul. His will is good and true and those who possess Him need nothing else. God's will is all powerful and wise. Those who trust completely without reservations have firm confidence and faith in Him. Do not seek other things or try to link events with God's designs, but surrender to Him blindly and with confidence. All that is graced upon you will produce individual fruits. My little ones, my blessing is upon you in the Name of My Jesus. Thank you for responding to my call.

Message from Our Lord Through Fr. Jack:

My dear ones, I am with you this night so put all fear aside. I am with you; there is no need to be anxious. The division that My presence brought and still brings to you is the division of choice between God and the world. I present you to My Father. The reason that He sent Me was to tell you that He is your Father also, and this is where the division comes. My dear ones, there is only one God, My Father and I, His only Son, and Our Holy Spirit. As I present you to God Our Father, your hearts are blessed and strengthened. Thank you My dear ones for choosing God. Know that in this choice others will be divided from you, that I am with you. I always take you to My Father. You are not alone. I bless you this night with My mercy and My peace

Thursday, October 29, 1992

Our Lady's message through Gianna Talone:

My dear little children, constantly pursue my Son and you shall find Him. Be faithful, happy and seeking souls advancing after my beloved Son. Remain faithful at the foot of the cross. Increase your love and adoration to Him. Venerate Him in untiring pursuit through all the disguises. Pass through the shadows and veils which may try to hide the will of my Son. Follow Jesus. Love Him and pray with all your heart. Pray! Please pray. Much has been mitigated because of prayer and conversion. Continue. my little ones. Everything is contingent upon prayer. Thank you for responding to my call.

Our Lord's message through Fr. Jack:

my dear ones. I am here again this night with you to say very plainly and speak to your heart — know for certain that there is a war going on at this moment for your soul. The warfare is intense; and yet, my dear ones, it is so subtle that many are being lulled into a state of complacency. In this warfare I say to you there is nothing for you to fear. I am with you. but I beg you this night to stay with Me. Be with Me, for with Me there is peace for you. and there is strength and there is hope. The devil is trying in every way to lure you from Me to destroy you. If you stay with Me, you will never be destroyed. .As you stay with Me, you will be purified. I love you with My heart, and I bless you this night again with My mercy. Stay with Me and you will be saved.

Thursday, November 5, 1992

Our Lady's message through Gianna Talone:

My dear little children. praised be Jesus. My little ones, Jesus not only gives freedom but also new life, a life you cannot attain by your own efforts. Do not trust in your own weak desire to take you to God, but place all your trust and confidence in His desire for you. You must remove yourself from the tensions of control and surrender completely. Ground yourself firmly on His absolute goodness and fidelity and not on your own feelings.

I love you, my dear little ones. My Son loves you. He has allowed me to be here with you. It is my prayer for you that Jesus will bring you to perfect fulfillment in Him. Thank you for your response to my call.

Our Lord's message given through Fr. Jack:

My dear ones. I have come this night to where you are to tell you once again you are mine! My Father has given you to Me. My dear ones, in so many ways I see how lost you still are, so distracted, so put upon, still so worried. When you allow those things to overcome you, you are lost and you are isolating yourself. I am here with you now this night to tell you take courage when you are beset with worry, when you are distracted. when you are fearful. Come to Me in My Most Blessed Sacrament, and there you will not only find Me, but you will find your true self. I will be with you always. I am with you now.

I ask you to thank My Father and yours that He has allowed Me to be with you for such a time, in such a way. I love you. Please do not be lost. I give My blessing of mercy to you and to your loved ones.

Thursday, November 12, 1992

Our Lady's message through Gianna Talone:

My dear little children, learn to rely on God and not on yourself. He leads you towards the fullness of life, bringing freedom of spirit, peace and insight. You will have far greater joy if you are detached from this world's created realities. An unselfish heart knows this and has a pure love for others. The more you love one another, the more God is loved. Have a generous heart, a pure one, and take courage in facing life and its demands. You will find joy with a pure heart and enjoy life, both human and divine, because you will be relying on God, not yourselves. You will find joy in all that there is. I bless you, my little ones, and thank you for responding to my call.

Our Lord's message through Fr. Jack:

My dear ones, I am with you again this night as a grace from My Father, to remind you again that even in your trials and in your suffering you are not alone. You, My dear ones, who are giving your heart to My Father and your Father, are so often ridiculed. Know, My dear ones, that when this happens you are not alone. I hold you. I am with you. I see your struggles and this night I give you My courage. Know that they will not last forever.

You are dear, so dear to My heart. I, your Lord, thank you for truly following me. You will never be lost as you take My hand. I bless you with My mercy and My peace, and I give you this night My strength in the face of all adversity. You are now living already the kingdom of God within your heart.

Thursday, November 19, 1992

Our Lady's message received by Mary Cook:

My dear children, pray, pray, pray! There is still much healing that needs to take place in your hearts and souls. By prayer and listening to the words of my Son can your hurts be transformed into love. Oh children, you too can heal one another by reaching out in love. Reach out, my little ones, in love to the anger and hurts of your brothers and sisters. Then will you find peace in your world. I love you, my little ones, and I'm praying with you always.

Our Lord's message through Fr. Jack:

My dear ones. this is the time of your visitation. My Father is allowing Me to again be so present to you. My mother is always with you. My dear ones, this night I come to remind you of how close We are to you. You only need to open your heart — We are there! We are as close to you as your breath. We surround you with Our love and with Our protection. Feel Our presence with you, around you. within you. You have nothing to fear. Hold on to Us. Our love is with you — the love of My mother and My love, which is a reflection of the love of God Our Father for you. Peace, my dear ones. Do not be afraid. We are with you! WE ARE WITH YOU!!

Thursday, December 3, 1992

Our Lady's message received by Gianna Talone:

My dear children, I am your mother who loves you, and I am here because of my Son. I thank you for your commitment to prayer in remaining faithful to my Son's request. My little ones, conversion takes time and my Son is so very patient. Be at peace to know He is with you, guiding you, and know His hand is so gently upon you. God, in His mercy, is so good and loves you abundantly. Do all that you can to focus on Him, surrendering daily to His will. Be at peace but never cease praying. The Lord is pleased with your prayer because you bring to Him in prayer so many special loved ones. God needs your prayers, your surrendering and openness.

I celebrate with you in prayer for your dedication and faithful commitment. Please unite with me for all those who choose not to follow His way. I need your prayers, my little ones, and there are so many special people searching and so confused. Join me in my quest for unity and happiness for all. I bless you and thank you for responding to my call.

Our Lord's message through Fr. Jack:

My dear ones, I come to you this night to thank you for listening and for responding to the request of My mother, which is My request also, for prayer. Thank you for your faithfulness. My dear ones, in the eyes of the world it is an accomplishment to pray as you have prayed for these 5 years but, my dear ones, it truly is such a small amount of time. But even with this small amount of time what your prayers are accomplishing is beyond the scope of your world. Know that your prayer matters. Continue to pray. I see you. I love you, and again this night My mother and I bring you to the throne of My Father. In gratitude, I bless you with My mercy and with My peace, and with the gift of perseverance from the Holy Spirit. Pray as you have been praying and know that your prayers are being answered.

Thursday, December 10, 1992

Our Lady's message through Gianna Talone:

My dear children, this night I come in the name of my Son to bestow upon you special blessings for your commitment in prayer to Him. I thank you, my dear little ones. I know how much you suffer, but I ask that you offer your suffering to my Son and rejoice in your living faith of His truth. My dear children, please continue to pray and to unite here in this place of my Son's divine mercy. Be supportive of my priests and my Son 's Church, be obedient to Our Pope, and know they have suffered also very much for my Son. Please pray for the Church to prevent division. Love and mercy cannot exist where there is division. I love you, my little children, and thank you for responding to my call.

* * * * * * * * * * * *

My dear ones, this is indeed the time of My Father's mercy for you. He sends Me. He allows Me to be with you in this way, to call you again to Him. I am now with you. My Father wishes you to believe that you are not alone. In this time My Father gives you many graces.

My dear ones, I ask you this night to accept these graces from Him - joy, hope, perseverance, and compassion. If you accept these graces, these gifts, My Father will be able to touch so many through you. Do not focus on your failings but upon God's mercy, upon My love for you. I give you the blessing of My mercy this night and the encouragement of Our Holy Spirit to continue listening as I speak continually to your heart. I give you also this night My peace.

Thursday, December 17, 1992

Our Lady's message through Gianna Talone:

My dear little children, during this Season I wish to celebrate with you my joy. The greatest gift I have to you is the gift of my Son, your Jesus. My dear little ones, on this night your sufferings will be lifted to my Son and will rest in His Most Sacred Heart. You, my little ones, can experience the joy of my Son, a Christmas day, everyday, if you unite and seek Him only. Oh, the joy of Him who reigns in the world. He is your peace and comfort. No gift is greater than my Son. I love you, my little ones, and I share with you my most precious love — my Son. Pray and prepare, for this time is a time of grace. Put aside all anxieties and stressful circumstances and see my Son there in your midst. Focus on Him, tend to Him and RE-JOICE! I love you and I celebrate with you your 5 years. Bless you and thank you for your response to my call.

Our Lord's message through Fr. Jack:

My dear ones, as you again, in a very few days, celebrate My birth, My Father again sends Me to you. I have been called by many titles, but the one I encourage you to embrace is Emmanuel — God with you. I am that gift given to you by God. My Father. I am always with you. From that moment that I was given life through My mother, Mary — Emmanuel, God with you. You are not alone. I, the Son of God, am always with you. The gift, a gift from a God — the God who loves you. That love is poured out on you through Me, through My birth, through My life, through My death, and through My Resurrection. I am your gift from God. And so this night I, the gift from God, give you, each of you, My peace, My strength, and I assure you again of My continuing presence, my real presence with you! I love you. I am with you. I am EMMANUEL!

Thursday, January 7, 1993

Our Lady's message received by Gianna Talone:

My dear little children, praise be Jesus. I rejoice in Him for allowing me to be here with you.

My dear ones, I wish for you only to focus on my Son, and seek His acceptance first and not of others. My little ones, only Jesus has a plan so beautiful and pure in His faithfulness for you. Do not be distracted by the words of others, but look to God to fulfill you and guide you. You all need each other, but only in Jesus can His plans be fulfilled in each of you. Jesus has a great plan of love and peace and freedom for all of you. Look to His love. Surrender and love Him. I love you, my little ones, but I urge you to be so secure in my Son that the words of others will not take you from that what my Son has planned for you. In Him all of you will be united in harmony and love. Praise be Jesus, my little ones. Pray! Pray! Pray to my Son.

I bless you and thank you for responding to my call. Serve God first and then you will be able to serve each other.

Thursday, January 14, 1993

Our Lady's message received by Gianna Talone:

My dear little children, in these times of struggle and economic disasters, I wish you to know of the great love my Son and I have for you. My little ones, procure your relationship with God now. Do not wait. I am confident in my Son that here, the center of His Divine Mercy, His people will be strong in faithfulness to Him. Faith in God is the only means to salvation and prayer is the way to purity and holiness. Only God can merit you with this grace, but your surrender to Him is the gateway to your total joy and protection.

Pray with me, my little ones. I need desperately your prayers for peace in this world. I love you and bless you in the name of He who has sent me. Thank you for responding to my call and the call of my Son. Peace.

Our Lord's message through Fr. Jack:

My dear ones, I ask you this night to truly listen and to trust Me, who gave My life for you, and for whom I was raised up by My Father. You trust Me only partially. My dear ones, if you still keep the control of your life, you block My will for you. Trusting means giving up to God all of who you are. When you trust, then you will be able to listen. When you do not trust, you are afraid to listen because you are afraid of what I may ask you. Trust Me when I say I wish only good for you. I am with you. I invite you again to begin anew — to trust. Trust so that you may truly listen and, as you listen, you will indeed hear Me.

I love you and I bless you this night with My mercy and with My peace.

Thursday, January 21, 1993

Our Lady's message received by Gianna Talone:

My dear little children. I am your mother of God here to tell you that the greatest love story is contained in the Sacred Host. When you receive your Jesus. open your hearts and your minds in purity allowing my Son to permeate every cell in your being. I love you, my dear ones, but only through trust and love can you grow in holiness. Only in my Son can you grow in holiness. Only He can merit you with the graces of love and trust. Faith is a gift to you. Please pray and never lose faith. No matter what devastations are in the world - never lose faith. Trust my Jesus. trust your Jesus. He is yours. Bless you, my little ones. Thank you for responding to my call.

Our Lord's message through Fr. Jack:

My dear ones, I come this night to remind you once again that I am with you and that I love you. I see your hearts. I see that you wish to give them to Me but I also see fear, and wondering, and questioning. My dear ones, please know that I love you beyond what you can ever grasp, and that I cherish each of you and bring you to My Father. I tell you, hold on. I give you this night the grace of My perseverance. I encourage you not to give up, not to look at yourself, but to look at Me. Everything will be alright. There is no need to worry. I am with you. I am walking with you these days. Peace I give to you. Peace!

Thursday, January 28, 1993

Our Lady's message received by Mary Cook:

My dear children,. I am your mother who comes to be with you this night. Oh my dear ones, I see your struggles and I ask you this night to pray for peace in your hearts. Pray to be able to accept change in your life. I ask you to pray for acceptance in the will of God in your life. I am always with you. I love you, my dear little ones. Peace to you!

Our Lord's message through Fr. Jack:

My dear ones, I come to you this night to ask you not to try to understand the will of My Father in your life, but simply to trust. 1 know, my dear ones, how incredibly hard that must seem to you for I, your Lord, in My humanness was tempted also, but I ask you to follow the example that I gave and to trust. I am walking with you so there truly is nothing to fear. This night I call you to trust and I, your Lord. see that so often in your attempt to understand you leave the will of My Father and begin to interpret what you think is His will. Come to Me as I am with you in My most Blessed Sacrament, and trust. You are so close. Don't give up. You will see why I called you to trust. This night I give you my courage. Hold on to Me within your heart. All will be well. I tell you all is well within you even now!

Thursday, February 4, 1993

Our Lady's message received by Gianna Talone:

My dear little children, I am here with you because of my Son's great love and mercy. I will continue to be with you as you continue to give of yourselves to your family and your brethren. My little ones, if you feel nothing, are alone or feel abandoned, know that it is in your nothingness that you are everything in my Son. It is in your ordinariness that you are extraordinary. My little ones, please trust in my Son. Be simple, loving and kind disciples of my Son. Focus on Him. Pray! Use the Sacrament of Reconciliation, fast and give to my Son what He has given to you. He loves you. He needs you. I need you. I love you and am here to unite all in His love. Bless you, my little ones. Bless you. Thank you for responding to this call. Focus on Him. Fight the evil one with love of yourself, your family and brothers and sisters. Fight with love and forgiveness. Peace!

Our Lord's message through Fr. Jack:

My dear ones, I am with you always. In each step of your journey I am there. I speak to you this night of My Father, who is also your Father. My dear ones, He is not a wrathful God. How could a wrathful God love you so much as to send you His only Son to save you. Would a wrathful God send you His Holy Spirit who will always be with you? My Father loves you. I am here again with you this night to say to you one more time — God does not want to be distant from you. My dear ones, He sends Me to you. I am with you. Look at Me! See Me within your hearts. I give you My peace. I give you My healing. There is no need of fear. Look at Me! I am your light! I am your safety! I am the Son of God for you, given to you. Be at peace! Be at peace!

Thursday, February 11, 1993

Our Lady's message received by Gianna Talone:

My dear little children, I love you and come in the name of Jesus. Praise Jesus. Praise my Son, my little ones. I once again wish to say to you that if you cannot truly trust unconditionally in my Son, then you cannot truly believe that God exists. It is through my Son that all joy, peace, harmony and the virtue of love can exist. My little ones, if you love you will trust, hope and endure. Please, my little ones, God loves you and through His Sacred Heart will you grow in holiness. TRUST HIM! Take the risk you see it as, and step out into His arms. He is there to guide you. Do not be afraid to give yourself unconditionally to my Son. Do not be afraid. You will be secure and live in joy and tranquillity. Bless you, my dear ones. Thank you for responding to my call.

Our Lord's message through Fr. Jack:

My dear ones, you are children of My Father. He has not abandoned you. He sends Me to you and My mother to remind you of the great gift in the inheritance which is yours. My dear ones, so often through fear you live as orphans and as a homeless person not knowing where you belong. Again I remind you, you are children of God and your home is with Him no matter how difficult the journey. Know that this is just the journey, not your home. You were created and are still being created in the image of My Father, of Myself and of Our Holy Spirit. My dear ones, this creating requires time as you look upon it. Look with My Father. He is instantaneous. This night I give you My strength for the journey. My peace I give you. I and My mother are with you each step of your journey. Persevere! We are with you!